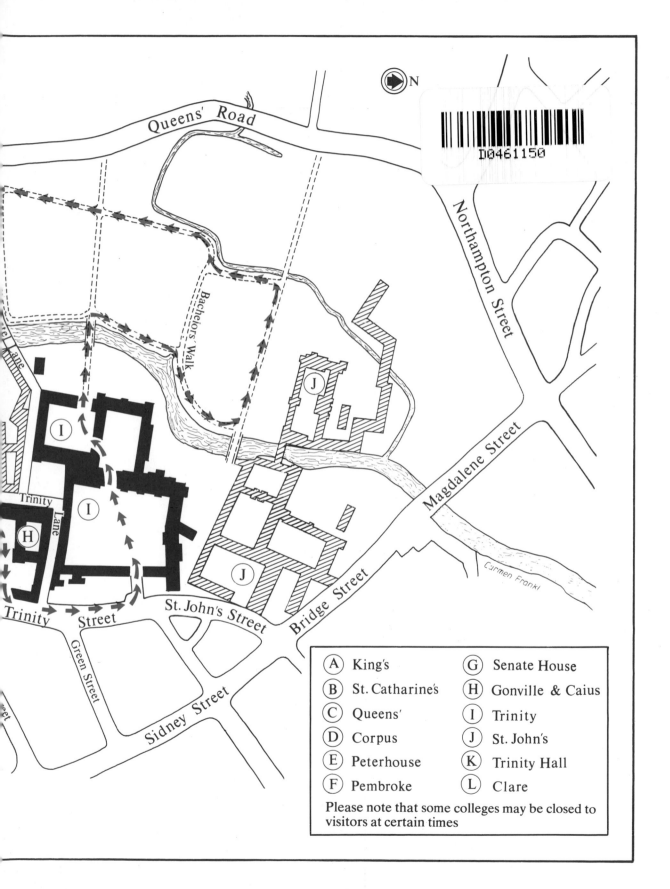

Queens' Road

Northampton Street

D0461150

Bachelors' Walk

Magdalene Street

J

Carmen Frankl

I

I

Trinity

Trinity Lane

H

St. John's Street

Bridge Street

Trinity Street

Green Street

J

Sidney Street

(A)	King's	(G)	Senate House
(B)	St. Catharine's	(H)	Gonville & Caius
(C)	Queens'	(I)	Trinity
(D)	Corpus	(J)	St. John's
(E)	Peterhouse	(K)	Trinity Hall
(F)	Pembroke	(L)	Clare

Please note that some colleges may be closed to visitors at certain times

N

CAMBRIDGE

CAMBRIDGE

and surrounding places of interest

Text by
MICHAEL HALL

With photographs by
ERNEST FRANKL

THE PEVENSEY PRESS
Cambridge England

Front cover Clare College and King's College Chapel from Clare Bridge

◄ *(Frontispiece)* **1** Graduates in formal academic dress outside the Senate House, where degrees are conferred

Back cover Queens' College Mathematical Bridge: a copy of the original of 1749–50

Published by The Pevensey Press
6 De Freville Avenue, Cambridge CB4 1HR, UK

Photographs: Ernest Frankl, except 7: Gerald Bye, courtesy of the Syndics of Cambridge University Library; 21: by permission of the Syndics of the Fitzwilliam Museum, Cambridge; 41: Edward Leigh, courtesy of the Provost and Fellows of King's College; 64: Gerald Bye, courtesy of the Librarian, Trinity College; 73: Edward Leigh, courtesy of the Master and Fellows of Trinity College; 74: Edward Leigh, courtesy of the Master and Fellows of Emmanuel College

Maps: Carmen Frankl

The assistance of Professor Sir Brian Pippard, Dr M.E. Smith and Dr S.M. Walters is gratefully acknowledged

Edited by Ruth Smith

Design by Tim McPhee
Design and production in association with Book Production Consultants, Cambridge

First published 1980
Second edition 1981
Third edition 1982
Fourth edition 1987

ISBN 0 907115 39 X hard covers
ISBN 0 907115 40 3 paperback

Typesetting in Baskerville by Westholme Graphics

Printed in Hong Kong

Contents

1 TOWN AND GOWN   1

2 UNIVERSITY BUILDINGS   15

3 THE COLLEGES   27
    Christ's College   27
    Clare College   31
    Corpus Christi College   32
    Downing College   34
    Emmanuel College   35
    Gonville and Caius College   37
    Jesus College   41
    King's College   44
    Magdalene College   51
    Pembroke College   53
    Peterhouse   56
    Queens' College   59
    St Catharine's College   61
    St John's College   63
    Sidney Sussex College   68
    Trinity College   69
    Trinity Hall   71
    19th- and 20th-century colleges   75

4 LIFE IN THE MODERN UNIVERSITY   83

5 PLACES OF INTEREST NEAR CAMBRIDGE   90

1 Town and Gown

Cambridge is world famous as the home of one of the two oldest English universities, but the city also has a long and eventful history of its own. From the earliest times its site was attractive, as a point at which a navigable river could be forded and bridged. It was also at the intersection of two major lines of communication, between the Thames valley and the Norfolk coast and from East Anglia to the Midlands, the only route avoiding the inhospitable fenland to the north and the dense forest to the south. In addition, the loop in the river and the surrounding marshland made any settlement relatively defensible.

There is evidence of uninterrupted human activity on or near the site of Cambridge from Neolithic times; relics of pre-Roman Cambridge can be seen in the University's Museum of Archaeology and Anthropology. When the Romans arrived here they may have bridged the river (as part of a road from Colchester to Lincoln) and by AD 43 had established a settlement – perhaps a staging-post for legions campaigning in the north. The Roman camp, thought to have been called Durolipons, was based on the north bank of the river (on the present Castle Hill) and was fortified. Besides being an important local administrative centre it was evidently prosperous, with substantial villas on both sides of the River Cam.

When the Romans left, the native British let the buildings of Durolipons decay. According to Bede (late 7th century) monks from Ely went to the ruined settlement and found there a marble coffin that they used for the burial of St Etheldreda, foundress of their monastery. Revival began with Offa the Great, who probably directed the building or rebuilding of the bridge at the end of the 8th century. At this time the town was called 'Grantacaestir', i.e. a fort on the Granta (the river's other name). However in 875 the *Anglo-Saxon Chronicle* calls it Grantabrycge – one of the earliest known uses of the word 'bridge' in the English language, suggesting that the town was famous for its bridge, and for the trade that bridges attract. It was controlled by the Danes until 921 and reached its peak of pre-medieval prosperity under King Edgar (956-75), when it was a noted county and market town with a mint, as important as the other East Anglian centres Norwich and Ipswich. In 1010, after a heroic resistance, Cambridge was captured by Viking marauders and razed to the ground. It is perhaps a sign of the town's earlier prosperity that it recovered rapidly: trade was thriving again well before 1066, and there is evidence of wealth in the numerous Saxon grave-slabs of very high quality that have survived.

In Saxon times there were flourishing communities on both sides of the Cam. The one on Castle Hill remained the seat of government, but the south-bank

◄ 2 *King's College Chapel looming over the rooftops of old Cambridge, a view that recalls the early uneasy relationship between town and gown*

community, on Peas Hill and Market Hill, was the more prosperous. These two 'hills' now appear no higher than their surroundings; in modern Cambridge 'hill' often denotes little more than an enclosed open space. The south bank was the busier because, with its numerous wharfs, it had better facilities for docking the barges which carried goods to Cambridge. Except for **St Peter's**, Castle Hill (**3**), the churches with Saxon origins are on the south bank. St Clement's, Bridge Street, predates even the Saxons, being a probably Danish foundation. St Botolph's, Trumpington Street (perhaps founded by the Ely monks) and St Edward's, between King's Parade and Peas Hill (dedicated to the Anglo-Saxon king and martyr) both date from Saxon times, but **St Bene't's** (i.e. St Bene-dict's) in Bene't Street alone retains some Saxon architecture (**4**). Its tower, the oldest building in Cambridgeshire, was erected in 1025; some portions of the original nave and chancel also remain. The most notable feature of the interior, the tower-arch, incorporates two carved lions, which are contemporary with the many Anglo-Saxon manuscripts in the library of Corpus Christi – the neighbouring college, which used St Bene't's as its chapel until the 16th century.

In 1068 William the Conqueror, journeying south after making peace with King Malcolm of Scotland, visited Cambridge. To consolidate his power over the region he had a castle built on what is now Castle Hill; it was initially of wood and erected on a steep mound, which still exists. It was reconstructed in stone by Edward I (1284) and occasionally provided royal lodgings, but by the 16th century it was in ruins and its stones were used in the building of King's College. After being repaired to serve as a barracks and then a prison it was finally demolished in 1842.

The prosperity of Norman Cambridge is suggested by the number of early-12th-century religious foundations: St Radegund's Priory (later Jesus College), St John's Hospital (later St John's College) and perhaps the most famous Cambridge church, the Church of the Holy Sepulchre (**6**), known as the **Round Church** (Bridge Street). One of the five surviving round churches in England, its shape was perhaps modelled on the slightly earlier round church at Northampton. The chancel, north chapel and south aisle are 15th-century additions to the round nave.

Cambridge's economic welfare was much strengthened by Stourbridge Fair, already well established by the early 13th century and by the 17th century the largest fair in England, visited by merchants from all over Europe. It took place during August and September on Stourbridge Common, east of the town, and is mentioned in *A Tour through . . . Great Britain* by Defoe, who devotes more space to it than to the University. The fair declined in the 18th century and in 1934 was abolished, leaving only such street-names as Garlic Row and Cheddars Lane to record its past importance.

The town reached the limits of its pre-19th-century expansion in the 1200s, when it was a small busy market town with the narrow, crooked streets it still retains, providing an outlet for the surplus grain produced by fertile Cambridgeshire and for the many goods unloaded at its port. Most of the houses had timber frames and clay-and-reed walls; one-storied cottages had walls of mud. All were thatched and fire was a constant hazard: St Bene't's suffered badly when the houses alongside it burnt down. Despite the almost total absence of local building stone, there were surprisingly many stone houses, indicating the wealth of individual families. One such house, Dunningstede, rebuilt in the late 12th century by Hervey Dunning, the town's first elected mayor, survives in the

►**3** *St Peter's, Castle Hill, traditionally founded in Saxon times on the site of a Roman temple of Diana; the earliest parts of the building and its fine font are Norman*

◄ **4** *The tower of St Bene't's, seen from Free School Lane; in the foreground are the medieval buildings of Corpus Christi College and* (centre) *the 16th-century gallery linking church and college*

grounds of St John's College with the fanciful name of the **School of Pythagoras** (**5**).

The beginning of the 13th century was also a turning-point in the town's history: the first scholars arrived and the University was established. The University's origins are obscure. In an attempt to outdo the claims of Oxford to greater antiquity, 16th-century Cambridge University historians claimed the legendary Spanish Prince Cantaber as their founder. He supposedly married the daughter of the king of the Britons in the year 4321 (calculated from the creation of the world) and brought to his city on the banks of the Cam astronomers and philosophers from Athens. The truth is more prosaic: in 1209 a band of scholars fled from riots in Oxford and established themselves here, though why they chose Cambridge is not clear. Probably some scholars already lived in the town, perhaps attached to the religious foundations. Almost from the very beginning, however, there was trouble; the refugee scholars did not find the calm they lacked in Oxford. While the townspeople were determined to exact fair rents and prices, the University was intent on protecting its members from being overcharged, and constantly interfered in the fixing of prices for goods, a matter which the townspeople naturally regarded as their prerogative. In 1231 Henry III forbade the University towns to exact exorbitant rents from scholars; this was the town's first taste of the power of the University when it had royal backing. The existence of the University in its midst was a real threat to the town, for 13th-century England was not a consumer society; the economy depended on people exchanging their own produce, and the town's growth may have been severely limited by the influx of a large number of scholars, who might spend much, but who produced nothing tangible.

▼ **5** *The 12th-century 'School of Pythagoras', one of the town's earliest domestic buildings and now a part of St John's College*

The scholars were often very unruly. In 1261 townspeople were involved in a riot between north- and south-country students, and 16 townsmen were hanged as a result. The University officials openly despised the mayor and corporation as uneducated bumpkins, easily outwitted by the learned. By a royal charter of 1317 the mayor and the town bailiffs were obliged, on taking office, to swear to maintain the privileges of the University, an annual ceremony so hated by the townspeople that they called it 'The Black Assembly'. In 1349 Cambridge suffered its first serious outbreak of plague, and there were further epidemics in 1361 and 1369. Then in 1381 the Peasants' Revolt sparked off a general rising against the scholars, who were regarded as harsh landlords – for by now the newly established colleges owned large parts of the town, and the situation of the previous century respecting unfair rents had been reversed. The University charters were seized and burnt in the Market Place, and the mayor forced the University authorities to make a deed giving up all their privileges and promising to conform to the law and custom of the town. Royal retribution was severe. The king deprived the town's governing body of all rights to regulate weights and measures and the prices of food and drink and transferred them to the University, which kept them until the 19th century.

In the Middle Ages the University, which existed before any of the colleges, was no more than a guild of teachers with the power to award degrees. Medieval University life was very unlike that of today. Undergraduates (students who have not yet taken a degree) were much younger, beginning their courses at 14 or 15. A university education took seven years to complete, but few students finished the course. The entrance requirements were not high: reading, writing and basic Latin. Simple Latin formed the 'grammatica' – the first part of the 'trivium' or primary course of study – intended mainly for prospective school-masters, elementary students known as 'glomerels' who were supervised by a man called the master of glomery. In the major part of the trivium the student learnt the arts of grammar, logic and rhetoric; of these logic was the most important since it provided grounding for the disputations, formal public arguments which took place in the University Schools and constituted the central element of medieval university education (they survived until the 18th century). In their second year students were allowed to take part in such disputations, being examined by the master (head) of their hostel or college. At the end of the Middle Ages, this was sufficient qualification for the degree of Bachelor of Arts, which completed the trivium. Finally study of the 'quadrivium' – arithmetic, music, astronomy and geometry – entitled the student to the degree of Master of Arts. He then had the choice of studying theology, civil law or canon (church) law, all of which led to well-paid professions.

To qualify for residence in the University students had to enrol on the matriculation list of a master within 15 days of coming to Cambridge. The first students lived in ordinary lodging houses, but gradually hostels were created especially for them. Students living in hostels paid for their own board and lodging, were governed by a principal and were supervised by the University authorities. In 1284 Hugh of Balsham founded Peterhouse, the first self-contained society of scholars – the first college. Most medieval undergraduates lived in hostels even after colleges were founded, for the colleges were primarily societies of teachers without responsibility for students, but by the late 15th century and largely emulating William of Wykeham's New College at Oxford, colleges were founded for societies of students and teachers living together, and

6 The Round Church, Bridge Street: the Norman design is preserved despite extensive 19th-century restoration

Here begynnyth the Pardoner his tale

the collegiate system which has survived until the present day was established. Thus there was a division of responsibilities: the University arranged teaching and awarded degrees, whereas the colleges provided board and lodging and, eventually, private tuition. The colleges were often founded or endowed by wealthy benefactors, but the University, with few independent sources of income, was poor. The townspeople were quick to notice the gradual transition from hostels to colleges. They complained that when the scholars lived in hostels they bought their provisions locally, but now that they lived in colleges they made their own bread and beer, had their own hythes (docks) along the river and bought in food from far away. The establishment of the first colleges coincided with the beginning of the eclipse of Cambridge as a port by King's Lynn.

It was not until the 14th century that the University began to change the appearance of Cambridge. In 1275 it bought the land on which the Old Schools were later built. During the first great period of college foundations (1324-52) seven new colleges were created. Of these, Clare Hall (later Clare College), Gonville Hall (later Gonville and Caius College), Trinity Hall and the two colleges later merged into Trinity, Michaelhouse and King's Hall, together formed a new University area between Trinity Lane and the river. King's Hall was the most flourishing because it enjoyed royal patronage. The single most spectacular alteration to the town's topography began in 1440, when Henry VI started to acquire land for King's College. His new foundation was so extensive

▲ 7 The Pardoner on his horse: a folio from the University Library MS Gg 4 27 (15th century) of Chaucer's Canterbury Tales, *a representative of the library's wealth of medieval manuscripts. Chaucer knew Cambridge well;* The Reeve's Tale *is set in the town and nearby Trumpington*

► 8, 9 Two historic Cambridge inns: above, the Fort St George on Midsummer Common; below, the yard of the Eagle, Bene't Street – latterly famous as the resort of Crick and Watson in the 1950s, at the time of their momentous discovery of the structure of DNA

that whole streets were wiped out, including an important access to the river which the king replaced with Garret Hostel Lane. In effect, Henry obliterated a quarter of the whole town (**2**). The second series of college foundations (1496-1594) was less devastating because the new colleges tended to take over the sites and buildings of defunct religious houses, many of which had been dissolved by Henry VIII. In this period the last of the hostels disappeared as the colleges, now seeing themselves not just as homes for scholars but as teaching institutions, began to make provision for the lodging of undergraduates.

The influence of the European Renaissance was evident in the vigorous activity of the University at the beginning of the 16th century. For the first time in centuries extensive changes were made in the curriculum. Erasmus lived in Cambridge between 1511 and 1514, and helped to initiate the study of Greek, biblical scholarship and the reading of classical authors other than Aristotle (the standard author for medieval scholars). Cambridge became a centre of advanced religious views; many of the most famous Protestant reformers, including Cranmer, Latimer and Ridley (all later martyred in Oxford by the Catholic Queen Mary), were educated here. Mathematics assumed a new importance. The University made great efforts to establish an adequate library of its own (as distinct from the colleges' libraries), and made large contributions towards the building of Great St Mary's Church (**15**).

Between 1610 and 1613 St John's and Trinity Colleges acquired land on the west side of the river, Trinity in exchange giving the town part of its common fields, Parker's Piece. This was the final great addition to the series of commons, such as Christ's Pieces, Jesus Green and Midsummer Common, which today still provide a ring of open spaces round the city and University centre. The

▼ **10** *Looking across the wide sweep of the Backs towards St John's New Building with the college's Tudor courts and 19th-century chapel on the right.*

11 *Spring on Trinity Backs, looking towards the Wren Library. The Backs are famous for their display of flowers in spring and early summer*

acquisition of land on the west side of the river, together with Clare College's acquisition of what is now its Fellows' Garden, was the beginning of **the Backs** – the land between the colleges and the river, first landscaped in the 18th century (**10**, **11**) – which complete the ring of open greenery.

The University suffered badly during the Civil War (1642-51). The town was Puritan and Parliamentarian, its MP being Oliver Cromwell himself; the University was largely Royalist and lost official favour during the Protectorate, indeed Cromwell put the heads of three colleges and Matthew Wren, bishop of Ely, in the Tower of London. However, with the Restoration of the monarchy, the University re-established its ascendency over the town. A new peacefulness characterises the history of Cambridge after 1700. Most domestic buildings in the centre belong to the early 19th century (**12**, **13**) but there are a few fine 18th-century town houses, such as Fitzwilliam House, Kenmare and the Master's Lodge of Peterhouse (all in Trumpington Street) and Little Trinity (Jesus Lane). Addenbrooke's General Hospital, founded by John Addenbrooke of St Catharine's, was erected between 1763 and 1766 in Trumpington Street (it now has a vast new site on the south side of the city). But while the town developed, the University declined. The new interest in scientific research, fostered by the presence of Isaac Newton in Cambridge at the end of the 17th century, now waned. No more colleges were founded and student numbers did not increase; teaching was leisurely and discipline slack.

There was increasing pressure on Cambridge and Oxford to expand and change during the 19th century. New subjects were taught, such as natural sciences and history, and the number of students slowly rose. Prince Albert, as University Chancellor (a position not usually marked by very active involve-

12, 13 *Early-19th-century Cambridge houses:* above, *cottages in Orchard Street;* below, *terraces in New Square*

14 *The colourful awnings of the stalls in the Market Square, seen from the tower of Great St Mary's*

ment in University affairs), did much to encourage the revival of university education. The town continued to develop: in 1845 the railway reached Cambridge, although (at the insistence of the University) the station was built far from the then centre of the town. In 1850 the corporation acquired a large area of the town centre by Act of Parliament, and the Market Square took on its present regular form. A new fountain replaced the conduit (1614) given to the town by Hobson, the famous carrier; the conduit was moved to its present site at the corner of Lensfield Road near the watercourse which originates in Nine Wells (Shelford Parish) and feeds the ponds and swimming pools of Emmanuel and Christ's Colleges as well as the Market Square fountain. The open gutters running with water in Trumpington Street are survivals of the original open watercourse.

Old disputes between town and gown were finally settled by Act of Parliament in 1856. The University lost its power to license alehouses and supervise weights and measures, markets and fairs, and the Black Assembly was abolished. The almost total dependence of the town's economy upon agriculture had ended with the enclosures of the early 19th century; the coming of the railway stimulated industry and Cambridge's suburbs grew. The town became a city in 1951 and now has well over 100,000 inhabitants. Although there are many factories, including some of international standing (e.g. those producing electrical components and scientific instruments), it would be an exaggeration to describe Cambridge as an industrial city. But it is emphatically no longer ' a town within a University' (if it ever was). Although the University inevitably dominates most visitors' impressions of Cambridge, 'town and gown' still lead very independent existences.

13

2 University Buildings

◄ **15** *Great St Mary's, the University Church, mostly built in the 15th century. This view, from between the Senate House and the Old Schools, emphasises the height of the tower, from which it is possible to see most of Cambridge*

OVERLEAF ►

16 (left) *The University Library (1934) is one of the nation's five copyright libraries; under the 1911 Copyright Act it is entitled to one copy of every book published in the United Kingdom*

17 (right) *Part of the view from Great St Mary's tower. In the foreground is the Waterhouse Building of Gonville and Caius College; beyond are Trinity College Great Gate and chapel, and in the distance the entrance gate and chapel tower of St John's College*

There is a great contrast between the wealth of college buildings already in existence by the late 16th century and the one modest quadrangle, dating from 1350, which was all that the University had been able to afford. This building, the **Old Schools** (**18**), still exists in a much altered form, opposite Great St Mary's Church. The side facing King's Parade was rebuilt in the 18th century, to complement the new Senate House.

In the Middle Ages the Old Schools housed the schools (i.e. faculties) of divinity, law and the arts, together with the **University Library.** The rapid growth of the Library, after the 18th-century Copyright Acts entitled it to one copy of every book published in Great Britain, meant that the Old Schools had to be expanded and new homes found for the faculties. In 1837 C. R. Cockerell designed a new building along Senate House Passage. Although it is plain on the outside, the interior is in the architect's most impressive monumental manner. By the 20th century space had run out and the Library moved (1934) to a vast new building across the river (**16**). A further extension has since proved necessary. In 1986 the Library contained more than 4,000,000 volumes.

After the departure of the Library from the Old Schools the law faculty returned to its medieval home and the rest of the quadrangle became the University State Rooms (not usually open to the public). To the west of the Old Schools is the old court of King's College which was sold to the University in 1829 and now houses its administrative offices.

Before the completion of the Old Schools most University activities took place in **Great St Mary's** (**15**), often known as the University Church. A church has stood on the present site since 1205. From the beginning it had a close connection with the new University. Charters and other important University documents were stored in it and, until the building of the Senate House, degrees were conferred there. The church was completely rebuilt between 1478 and 1519, mostly with University funds, though both Richard III and Henry VII also contributed. From the top of the tower (begun 1491, finished 1608) one can see most of Cambridge (**17**). It is a spacious Perpendicular church, typical of many built at this time throughout East Anglia, with its original timber roof (1506). The galleries in the aisles were inserted in 1736, to accommodate the undergraduates who came to hear the University sermons. The quarter-hour chimes of Great St Mary's clock, composed in 1793 by Joseph Jowett, professor of civil law, were copied in 1859 for the chimes of Big Ben at the new Houses of Parliament, and under the name of the 'Westminster Chimes' have been widely adopted throughout the world.

The **Senate House** (1722-30) was the first new University building for over two centuries (**18**). The architect was James Gibbs, who also designed King's College Fellows' Building and the Church of St Martin-in-the-Fields at the corner of Trafalgar Square, London. Originally it was intended as only one side of a whole quadrangle, but no more was built. Inside there is much fine woodwork and a lavish plasterwork ceiling, all 18th-century. The University's chief ceremonial functions, such as the conferring of degrees, all take place here. The cast iron railings which surround the Senate House were some of the first to be erected in England. The Senate House is the sole fragmentary realisation of the schemes for remodelling the centre of Cambridge proposed by the 18th-century architects Hawksmoor, Gibbs and Adam. Hawksmoor's plan involved demolishing much of central Cambridge and replacing it with a series of avenues and piazzas. Even if the money had been available for such an expensive scheme, it might well have been objected to as a design more worthy of Louis XIV than of an English university.

Instead there was no further building until the 19th century, and even then the initiative did not come from the University. In 1804 it was offered the

▼**18** *18th-century University buildings: left, the east front of the Old Schools, which houses the University's administrative offices; right, James Gibbs' Senate House*

surplus from public subscriptions raised to finance a statue of William Pitt (Prime Minister 1783-1805), in order to erect a new building for the **University Press** near Pembroke College, where Pitt had studied. The result was the Pitt Press (1833) on Trumpington Street, a pretty Gothic building with a fine tower which often leads it to be mistaken for a church. The history of printing in Cambridge is of course much older than the Pitt Press. The first Cambridge book was printed privately in 1521, and in 1534 Henry VIII granted the University a charter to print and sell books. Cambridge University Press shares with its Oxford counterpart the privilege of printing prayer books and bibles; the Folio Bible, printed in 1763 by the famous University printer Baskerville (who also designed the type used in this guidebook), has often been described as one of the most beautifully printed books in the world. The Press acquired new buildings near the railway station in the 1960s, extending them in the 1970s to house all its operations. It is now a major printing and publishing business, but remains under the direct control of the University.

Near the Pitt Press can be seen the result of an even more munificent donation, the **Fitzwilliam Museum.** In 1816 Viscount Fitzwilliam bequeathed to the University his collection of paintings, manuscripts, books and engravings, together with £100,000 to build a museum in which to house them. This was designed by George Basevi, who was killed in a fall from Ely Cathedral before the Museum was finished. The exterior is a dramatic, almost baroque, 19th-century interpretation of the classical temple façade; its impressive colonnaded portico is flanked by flights of steps and imposing pairs of lions (**20**). The entrance hall and main galleries are probably the most ornate rooms in Cambridge. Viscount Fitzwilliam's collection has been greatly added to, as has the original building. Besides antiquities of Greece, Rome, Egypt and the Near and Far East, the Museum has an extensive collection of applied arts of all periods, notably armour and ceramics (**21**). The library contains many hundreds of illuminated manuscripts as well as literary and musical autographs, including the first draft of Keats' 'Ode to a Nightingale'. The collection of paintings has

examples of all the major European schools including outstanding works by Simone Martini, Domenico Veneziano, Titian, Tintoretto and Veronese of the Italians; Hogarth, Blake, Constable and Augustus John of the English; Rubens, Van Dyck and Frans Hals of the Flemish and Dutch; and Degas and Monet of the French. Samples from the large collection of old master drawings are usually on display and there are also temporary exhibitions.

In the late 19th century the University began a great burst of building activity, partly because of changes in the curriculum. In the early 1800s the Cambridge undergraduate, if he studied at all, received a very narrow course of instruction, mainly in mathematics. Professors of other subjects did hardly any teaching; many lived away from the University. Oxford and Cambridge compared unfavourably with the more progressive universities of Edinburgh and London. Slowly changes were made; perhaps the most significant development was in the teaching of science. Provision for full-scale modern scientific teaching and research was beyond the resources of the colleges, so the University began to build the great conglomeration of lecture rooms and laboratories on the Downing Site between Downing College and Pembroke Street. This area also contains the scientific museums of the University which house its great collections of geology, archaeology and anthropology, and zoology. The old **Cavendish Laboratories** for physics were built on the site of the old Botanic Garden in Free School Lane (1872-3) at the expense of the Chancellor, the seventh Duke of Devonshire, of the Cavendish family. This is one of the most famous

▲ **20** *The lions outside the Fitzwilliam Museum, which houses the University's collection of art and antiquities*

► **21** *A sample of the Fitzwilliam Museum's treasures: a Chinese* famille rose *dish (1723-35) and bowl (1736-95). Ceramics so decorated were intended as gifts; the pattern symbolises the blessings that the donor wishes to bestow*

research institutions in the country, guided for many years by Lord Rutherford (Cavendish Professor of Physics 1919-37). Here in 1897 J. J. Thomson established the existence of electrons; his work in Cambridge won him the Nobel Prize (1906) and was continued by Sir James Chadwick, who identified the neutron, and by Sir John Cockcroft and E. T. S. Walton, who in 1932 achieved the artificial disintegration of nuclei. The new Cavendish Laboratories on the Madingley Road were opened in 1973; the work of the old laboratories is commemorated by a plaque on their buildings in Free School Lane. Close by is the Whipple Museum of the History of Science, housed in the Jacobean hall of the old Perse School, the 'free school' that gave the lane its name.

Not all late-19th-century scientific activity in Cambridge was centred on the Cavendish Laboratories. William Bateson, who became professor of biology in 1908, laid the foundations of modern genetics by continuing the hitherto neglected work of the Bohemian botanist Mendel. The **Botanic Garden** (**22**) has played an important part in the scientific work of the University. It was established (1762) by Dr Richard Walker, vice-master of Trinity College. The present site, on Trumpington Road, was purchased in 1831 and the first tree of the new Garden was planted in 1846. At first only one half, that nearest Trumpington Road, was laid out, with a pool, glasshouses and one of the first English rock-gardens; the rest was planted in the 20th century. The collection of trees and shrubs is exceptionally good and is arranged in systematic groups. The primary aim of the collections is to provide a range of material for teaching in the University courses, and there is an experimental area (not normally open to the public) in which plants are grown under controlled conditions. Increasingly the publicly displayed collections are used by schools and adult education groups, and the Garden is valued by the city and its visitors as a beautiful park.

Personal benefactions to the University have not entirely ceased. In 1967 H. S. Ede gave his house and art collection to the University. The house, at **Kettle's Yard** on Castle Hill (**23**), contains a large collection of 20th-century works, notably sculptures and drawings by Gaudier-Brzeska and paintings by Ben Nicholson, David Jones and Christopher Wood, displayed in a domestic setting. It has been extended with a gallery for temporary exhibitions, and in term-time it is used for regular chamber concerts.

Despite the rapid growth of the University from the mid 19th century, the decision to expand outside the city centre was not taken until the mid 20th century. Engineering Laboratories were moved to Fen Causeway (1948) and a new Chemistry Laboratory was built on Lensfield Road (1953-60), opposite the Scott Polar Research Institute (1934), which is named after the antarctic explorer and contains a small museum of the history of polar exploration. In 1955 a Veterinary School was opened. Astronomy has been studied at Cambridge for centuries; in 1706 the Plumian Professor of Astronomy constructed an observatory for himself on top of Trinity Great Gate. The observatory on the

▼ 23 Kettle's Yard House, which contains an extensive collection of 20th-century art, given to the University with the house by H.S. Ede

24 *Part of the University's Mullard Observatory radio telescope installation at Lords Bridge, near Cambridge*

◄**25** *The History Faculty building (1964-8), designed by James Stirling*

Madingley Road was built in 1822-3. In the 1960s a series of radio telescopes (**24**) was erected at Lords Bridge, west of Cambridge. It was here that the first pulsar was discovered. The extreme regularity of the received pulses soon convinced the astronomers that the signals were emitted by inanimate objects and not, as was conceivable, by aliens in outer space.

The University has also been concerned to establish facilities for the growing graduate population of Cambridge. The University Centre, overlooking the river near Silver Street, provides a social centre for graduates. A much admired piece of architecture, it was built between 1964 and 1967 to designs by Howell, Killick, Partridge and Amis. Good examples of other recent University buildings can be seen between Sidgwick Avenue and West Road in the faculties of English, modern and oriental languages, philosophy, classics, history and music. The History Faculty building (1964-8), designed by James Stirling, is one of the boldest and most controversial buildings ever erected in Cambridge (**25**).

Slowly the whole of west Cambridge, a pleasant area of Victorian villas, preparatory schools and playing fields, has changed its appearance. The many new buildings have reorientated the University, so that the Backs are now at its centre, and Cambridge, whilst clinging to its collegiate past, also assumes the aspects of a campus.

3 The Colleges

Christ's College

Christ's originated in a small college called God's House, founded in 1439 by William Byngham, a London parish priest, to train schoolmasters. At first it was close to the river, but when Henry VI decided to purchase its land for his own new college, King's, God's House had to move to a new site outside the town's Barnwell gate. In 1505 Lady Margaret Beaufort (who later founded St John's) assumed control of God's House, changed its name to Christ's College and began to enlarge its buildings and endowments. The present college probably incorporates some of the buildings of God's House, which would explain the irregularities in the buildings between the gatehouse and the chapel. The rest of the First Court was built in Lady Margaret's time; her coat of arms can be seen on the gateway over the entrance (**26**) and on the oriel window of the Master's Lodge (**27**). The whole court was refaced at intervals between 1758 and 1770, largely by James Essex, in a simple classical style; the result is very pleasing.

The care of her new college became the major interest of Lady Margaret's last years. She reserved rooms for herself and frequently came to stay. The statutes were probably drawn up mainly by her friend John Fisher, bishop of Rochester, but doubtless incorporate her own views about the running of the college; they give an interesting picture of 16th-century college life. The gates were to be locked at 9 p.m. in winter and 10 p.m. in summer. The master was paid £6 13s 4d per annum and had a clothes allowance of £1. Adult members of the college who misbehaved were to be fined but those under 21 were to be beaten. Fellows had to come to chapel in *clean* surplices, three times on Sundays and feast days and at least five times during the rest of the week. They were to teach theology, philosophy and the arts. Only Latin was to be spoken in college, except in a man's rooms or on holidays. Students were forbidden to take part in drinking parties, engage in trade, carry weapons, keep dogs or hawks or play with dice or cards except in the hall at Christmas. If the college launderer was a woman she had to be honest and of virtuous conversation. It is not possible to tell how many of these rules were observed when Lady Margaret was not present to keep things in order.

The Fellows' Building beyond the First Court was begun in 1640 – one of Cambridge's earliest examples of architecture in a classical idiom. Its design is traditionally, but without evidence, attributed to Inigo Jones. A local architect is more likely; there are similarities to those parts of Clare College known to have been designed by Thomas Grumbold. Behind the Fellows' Building is the

◄**26** *Christ's College main gate: above is the coat of arms of Lady Margaret Beaufort. The yales supporting the shield are mythical beasts, able to rotate their horns at will*

lovely Fellows' Garden (**28**) with its 18th-century bathing pool and garden house. In 1608 the college bought 300 mulberry trees to gratify James I's plans for an English silk industry, and the mulberry that still exists in the Fellows' Garden (and is traditionally associated with Milton) may be one of them. Milton was at Christ's between 1625 and 1632, his delicate and youthful appearance earning him the nickname of 'the lady of Christ's'. He wrote some of his early major poems here, including the 'Ode on the Morning of Christ's Nativity'. 'Lycidas' was written in memory of Edward King, a fellow of the college and a lecturer in Greek, and specifically refers to Cambridge, as do Milton's two poems 'On the University Carrier'. These concern Thomas Hobson (died 1631), a well-known local character who is supposed to have originated the expression 'Hobson's Choice' with his custom of making each of his clients hire the horse standing nearest the stable door.

In the 18th century the chapel was refitted, but the original timber ceiling was retained. The chapel contains the superb double monument to two fellows of the college, Sir John Finch and Sir Thomas Baines (1684). Finch was a professor at Pisa and subsequently ambassador to Constantinople; Baines was a doctor and his inseparable companion. Their portraits on the monument compare interestingly with those painted by Carlo Dolci, now in the Fitzwilliam Museum.

Charles Darwin, author of *The Origin of Species*, entered Christ's in 1825. His undergraduate career did not show great academic promise, but he formed some influential friendships, notably with Henslow, the professor of botany. He returned to Christ's as a fellow-commoner to write up the notes he had taken whilst voyaging with the *Beagle*.

20th-century building in Christ's extensive grounds includes a block of

►**28** *Christ's College: the gateway in the Fellows' Building leading to the Fellows' Garden*

▼**27** *Christ's College: the First Court, looking towards the Master's Lodge*

student accommodation and other facilities abutting King Street, designed by Denys Lasdun. It forms a dramatic climax to a walk through the college, but from the street appears crushingly arrogant.

Clare College

Because most of its buildings date from the 17th century it is easy to forget that Clare is the second oldest college. The site was acquired by the University in 1298 for the establishment of a University College like the one that still exists at Oxford. But at Cambridge the new college had inadequate endowments and rapidly declined. It was rescued by a remarkable woman, Lady Elizabeth de Clare, a granddaughter of Edward I. She was a close friend of the Countess of Pembroke, foundress of Pembroke College, and, like her, keenly interested in the furtherance of education. In 1338 she refounded University Hall as Clare Hall, the name by which the college was known until 1856. She wished her new college to provide education for poor boys as well as a home for teachers in Cambridge. At this early date such a conception of a college – a community of students and teachers living together – was highly unusual; it did not gain common acceptance until after the foundation of New College, Oxford, in 1379.

The original buildings were mainly burnt down in 1521, but a new court was quickly erected to replace them. These buildings would have been familiar to the famous Protestant reformer and martyr Hugh Latimer, a fellow of the college, and to Nicholas Ferrar, also a fellow, who established the religious community at Little Gidding which George Herbert and Charles I visited and T. S. Eliot celebrated in *Four Quartets*. By the beginning of the 17th century the new buildings were dilapidated and it was decided to rebuild the college. The bridge was constructed first, probably because building materials were to be carried over the river at this point. Designed by Thomas Grumbold, it is often reckoned to be the prettiest of the many bridges over the Cam (see front cover). It is an old joke to ask visitors to count the number of balls that surmount the bridge. The unexpected but correct answer is thirteen and four fifths: one has a segment missing.

Work began on the east range, fronting Trinity Lane, at the same time and finished in 1641. All further work was halted by the Civil War and was not resumed until 1662; it continued slowly until the completion of the Master's Lodge in 1715. But although the court took 80 years to build it forms a remarkably harmonious and well-proportioned whole (**29**), partly because of a general 'tidying up' in the 18th century. Alterations were obviously made to the design during the course of building; for instance, the east front is very different from the river front with its giant pilasters. Yet the building is pleasing from every angle, especially when seen across the lawns of King's (**42**).

The chapel was added between 1763 and 1769; the architects were Burrough and Essex. It is the only college chapel to have an octagonal ante-chapel, providing a dramatic and beautiful contrast to the chapel itself. Clare is famous for the beauty of its intricate 18th-century wrought iron gates at the bridge and at both entrances, and for its Fellows' Garden on the far side of the river, probably the loveliest of the Cambridge gardens regularly open to the public (**30**).

New buildings to accommodate increased numbers of students became an urgent necessity by the late 19th century. In 1922 work began on Memorial

◄ 29 *Clare College: looking across Old Court to the dining hall range; the cupola of the ante-chapel is visible on the right*

Court, on the far side of Queens' Road, financed by a fund commemorating members of the college killed in World War I. The architect was Sir Giles Gilbert Scott, who also designed the neighbouring new University Library. A new college library was built in the centre of the court in 1984-6. The college hostel on Chesterton Lane (1957-8) was designed by David Roberts.

Corpus Christi College

Corpus Christi is unusual in that it has no individual founder. It was founded by two Cambridge guilds, the Guild of Corpus Christi and the Guild of the Blessed Virgin Mary, and a royal licence was secured for it in 1352. The Guild of Corpus Christi was housed near the churchyard of St Bene't's, and the first buildings of the new college were erected close by. This relationship with the guilds, and hence with the town of Cambridge, explains why Corpus is the sole college to have its site in the heart of old Cambridge. The other colleges established at this time were either in the new University quarter that had sprung up by the river (including Clare, Trinity Hall and Gonville and Caius) or were outside the town boundaries (Pembroke and Peterhouse).

The college was so closely linked with St Bene't's that until the 19th century it was known as Bene't College; the church (**4**) served as the college chapel, and in 1500 a gallery, which still exists, was built connecting church and college, like that between Peterhouse and Little St Mary's. Cambridge townspeople for long regarded Bene't College almost as their own property. On the festival of Corpus frequently stolen or lost. He specified that the volumes were to be kept under

Christi the college had a procession, followed by a feast for townspeople who had taken part in it, and there was much discontent when the college discontinued the feast after Henry VIII had abolished the observance of Corpus Christi. The college was often at the centre of the strife between town and gown. In 1381 it had such a bad reputation as a harsh landlord that a mob broke in and carried off many of its valuables. A similar riot in 1688 was caused by the rumour that the college bursar was Roman Catholic.

No visitor to Cambridge should fail to visit the Old Court of Corpus Christi (**31**), the best surviving example of an early medieval college court (1352-78, with late-15th-century buttresses). In 1823 a large new court was built to the designs of William Wilkins, the architect of Downing College, containing the hall, library and chapel. The old hall, in the Old Court, became the college kitchens. The chapel contains some very fine 16th-century stained glass, apparently provided by Wilkins himself.

The chief treasure of the library is the great collection of books and manuscripts presented by Archbishop Parker (master 1544-53), most of which came from the libraries of monasteries dissolved by Henry VIII. Particularly notable is the 6th-century Canterbury Gospel, which is believed to have been given by Pope Gregory the Great to St Augustine. There are nearly 40 Anglo-Saxon manuscripts, among them the most important copy of the *Anglo-Saxon Chronicle*. Archbishop Parker was concerned that his library should be looked after as carefully as possible, knowing that books in 16th-century Cambridge were very

▼ **31** *Corpus Christi College: the Old Court (mostly 14th century). The ghost of Dr Butts (master of the college 1626-32), who hanged himself shortly before he was due to give the University sermon, has been seen leaning from one of the windows*

three locks and the keys held by the master and two fellows. The masters of Gonville and Caius College and Trinity Hall were to make an annual inspection, and if they found that a substantial amount of the library had been lost, the whole collection was to pass to Caius. If Caius was similarly careless, Trinity Hall could claim what remained. Parker also gave his college a good deal of silver, adding to a collection which contains what is probably the earliest piece of plate owned by any Cambridge college, a drinking-horn dated 1347.

Perhaps the most famous alumnus of Corpus Christi is Christopher Marlowe, Shakespeare's most powerful rival in the Elizabethan theatre. He is known to have had rooms in Old Court in 1578 and graduated MA in 1587, having already written his sensational play *Tamburlane*. An Elizabethan portrait, thought to be of Marlowe, was discovered behind wainscotting in the college in the 20th century and now hangs in the hall. Other famous writers who have studied at Corpus include the novelists John Cowper Powys and Christopher Isherwood.

Downing College

In 1717 Sir George Downing, baronet, left his property to his four cousins in succession with the remainder to be used for the founding of a new college at Cambridge. The last heir died in 1754 but the last Lady Downing, who had no intention of parting with the money, entered into prolonged and costly litigation to prove that the University had no claim. Although she lost her case she retained the Downing estates for her lifetime, and did all she could to ensure that should the University ever receive Sir George's gift it would be worth as little as possible, even having the Downing family mansion at Gamlingay, near Cambridge, demolished. Fortunately Lady Downing died in 1778, but her heir kept the property as long as he could. The college was not finally established until 1800 and the foundation stone was not laid until 1807.

The site was originally very large, but the northern part was sold to the University (1896-1902) to form the Downing Site, now occupied by museums and laboratories. Sir George's vast endowment was greatly reduced by the cost of litigation, so not all the college could be built at once. Indeed it did not reach anything that could be called a finished form until the 20th century, and Downing remains comparatively poor.

George III was of the express opinion that the buildings of the new college should not be Gothic. The architect, William Wilkins, perhaps influenced by this mandate, turned his back on the medieval college groundplan. Instead of creating enclosed courts he spaced out the college buildings, using a Greek classical idiom, around a large turfed central area. Thus he created the first campus, some years before the building of the first campus university at Virginia.

Wilkins designed the east and west wings; more was added in 1874, following his plans. In 1930 work was resumed, but whereas Wilkins had intended a large entrance gate in the middle of the northern area of the court, it was completely filled in (1953). However the southern side was left open, creating a spacious view, with the spire of the Victorian Catholic Church rising behind the trees. The combination of wide lawns and light-coloured Grecian buildings is very attractive (**32**). Downing's most recent addition is the Howard Building, a 200-seat auditorium in classical style by Quinlan Terry (1986).

A characteristic part of Downing College's spacious lawns and 19th-century Grecian buildings

The troubles that beset Downing's foundation were profitable only to the lawyers involved, so it is appropriate that the college is noted for its teaching of law.

Emmanuel College

Like Sidney Sussex and Magdalene, Emmanuel was established on the site of a religious house dissolved by Henry VIII in 1538. It had been occupied by Dominican friars since 1240. Despite the protests of the Vice-Chancellor, the property was not immediately converted to collegiate use but was sold into private hands. In 1583 Sir Walter Mildmay, Chancellor of the Exchequer under Elizabeth I, acquired it and established Emmanuel College a year later, 'with a design' (as he wrote) 'that it should be a seed-plot of learned men for the supply of the Church, and for the sending forth of as large a number as possible of those who shall instruct the people in the Christian faith. We would not have any Fellow suppose that we have given him in this College a perpetual abode . . .' Cambridge had been unable to provide the newly established Protestant church with the educated clergymen and preachers it needed, for the study of theology in the University was in serious decline; Emmanuel, in aiming to supply them, rapidly became the principal centre of Protestant theology in Cambridge. Inevitably it suffered during the high-church revival under Charles I, Archbishop Laud attacking its chapel services for irreligious informality. The many men of Puritan leanings who emigrated to the New World at this time included 35 educated at Emmanuel – more than from any other Cambridge college. Amongst them was John Harvard, who had entered Emmanuel in

1627. He emigrated in 1637 and at his death (1638) left half his estate and his library to a college to be established at New Town (later named Cambridge in memory of the University that had educated so many of the early immigrants) – the future Harvard University. A memorial plaque to John Harvard, presented by members of Harvard University, can be seen in Emmanuel chapel.

Initially the existing monastic buildings were absorbed into the fabric of Emmanuel, the friars' church being converted into a hall. This was completely refitted by James Essex, the fine 18th-century panelling and plasterwork concealing the great antiquity of the structure (**74**). The first major addition to the college after the founder's death was Brick Building (completed 1634), to the south of the main court. By this time the founder's chapel was looked on with disfavour; because of his Puritan sympathies he had built it orientated north–south instead of the usual east–west, and it had never been consecrated. William Sancroft, master from 1662 to 1664 and subsequently dean of St Paul's, entrusted the design of a new chapel to Christopher Wren, with whom he was in regular contact over the survey of the decayed old St Paul's Cathedral. Work began in 1668; the date 1673 above the pediment probably refers to the completion of the fabric. The fitting up of the interior, with its superb plasterwork and woodwork, began in 1676. The chapel was consciously modelled on Peterhouse chapel in its lay-out and siting in relation to the main court, and is constructed behind a long gallery set over an arcade. The façade is thus separate from the main body of the chapel. Unlike Wren's chapel at Pembroke it is not very classically correct in its details; for instance, the pediment is broken

▼33 *Emmanuel College: the chapel, designed by Sir Christopher Wren, and the long gallery over the arcade stand between First Court and the gardens*

by a clock surmounted by a tall cupola. The garlands around the clock and festoons between the pilasters and engaged columns give the whole a cheerful and festive appearance (**33**). At night, dramatically floodlit, the façade looks like the backdrop for a 17th-century masque. The old chapel became in turn a library and an extra dining hall.

The rest of the main court was rebuilt in the 18th century. A new south range, largely financed by Thomas Fane, sixth Earl of Westmorland, and named the Westmorland Building in his honour, was completed in 1722. The west range, facing St Andrew's Street, was completely rebuilt (1769-75) by James Essex. It now forms the main entrance to the college (**34**), which had previously been on Emmanuel Street. Emmanuel's grounds, incorporating a lake in which the fellows used to bathe and ornamental ducks now swim, are amongst the most attractive in Cambridge.

Gonville and Caius College

Gonville and Caius (conventionally just 'Caius') has two names because it was founded twice, in 1348 and again in 1557. The first founder, Edmund Gonville, was a priest and a close friend of Bishop Bateman, founder of Trinity Hall. Gonville died shortly after buying the original site (on Free School Lane) and Bateman, as executor of his will, was entrusted with money to enlarge and endow the new college. Having begun by moving the site to its present location, close to Trinity Hall, Bateman arranged a 'Treaty of Amity' between the two colleges (1353). Without his energetic support the new Gonville Hall would probably not have survived; nevertheless, it was not wealthy enough to erect

new buildings, and so existing houses on the site were converted to collegiate use. A chapel was in existence by 1393 but was very small, as was the first court to be built, now known as Gonville Court: despite the long time spent in its construction (1441-90), its area is only 26 m. square. Like many other Cambridge courts, it was entirely refaced in the 18th century, and now has a neat classical appearance.

Many Gonville Hall undergraduates lived in Physwick Hostel, on the far side of Trinity Lane. In 1546 Henry VIII incorporated the hostel into his new foundation, Trinity College (its site is now part of Trinity Great Court), leaving Gonville Hall in urgent need of new accommodation. Fortunately a man was on hand to provide it: John Caius (pronounced 'keys'), the college's second founder. He entered Gonville Hall as a student in 1529 (with the name of John Kaye, which he later latinised); subsequently he studied in Italy (1539-44), taking a medical degree at the famous University of Padua, and brought back to England medical knowledge far in advance of native doctors. In 1557 he obtained a royal charter of foundation for 'Gonville and Caius College' and became master two years later, completing the present site with the purchase of more land. He also added considerably to the college's endowments, making it one of the richer Cambridge colleges.

Besides this Caius financed the building of a new court, now named after him, for which he drew up most of the plans himself. Its south side, along Senate House Passage, was deliberately left open 'lest the air from being confined within a narrow space should become foul, and so do harm to us . . .' His medical training had given Caius a concern for hygiene which was far from common at his time. As well as introducing the pattern of the three-sided court – often imitated in other colleges – Caius gave directions in his will for keeping the college clean, leaving money to pay a man to clean the pavements and gutters outside and inside the college courts. He established the college's continuing reputation in the field of medicine; famous physicians who have studied at Caius include William Harvey, who discovered the circulation of the blood.

Caius' architectural designs included the three famous gates symbolically marking the steps of a student's career. The first gate, onto Trinity Street, was extremely simple and called Humility, the first stage in an academic career. Although the original gate now stands in the Master's Garden, the word HUMILITATIS can still be seen carved over the entrance to the college beyond the Porter's Lodge. Between Caius Court and Tree Court is the massive Gate of Virtue (1565-9). Finally the student passes through the most elaborate gate, that of Honour (1575), on his way to the Old Schools to sit his examination and receive his degree (**35**). The Gates of Virtue and Honour are remarkable as examples of classical architecture, which at the time of their building was almost completely unknown in England – an innovation presumably owing to Caius' experience of Renaissance architecture during his years in Italy.

◄ **35** *Gonville and Caius College: the 16th-century Gate of Honour, showing two faces of its unusual sundial, designed to give the time at different periods of the day. In the foreground are some of the cast iron railings that surround the Senate House*

Sadly, Caius' mastership of the college he did so much for was not happy. There was continual tension between his strong Catholic sympathies and the Puritan beliefs of most of the fellows. For long Gonville and Caius was known as a home of strongly Protestant views. In 1572 the fellows sacked Caius' rooms in the belief that he had stored 'Popish trumpery' there. Caius resigned a year later and died within a month. He was buried in the college chapel, where a splendidly elaborate monument (1575) was erected. The chapel contains two other fine monuments: to Stephen Perse MD (1615), founder of the Perse

◄ **36** *Jesus College: the chapel, once the church of St Radegund's Convent (founded in the early 12th century); the upper part of the tower is a 15th-century addition*

School, Cambridge, and Thomas Legge (1607), a master of the college.

The college has expanded considerably since the 19th century. Between 1868 and 1870 all the buildings in Tree Court were demolished and replaced with a large new building designed by Sir Alfred Waterhouse in his favourite French Renaissance style. Its tower, looking onto King's Parade, made it once the most despised building in Cambridge, but modern eyes can see it more dispassionately as typical of its age. Caius did much to regain its architectural good name with the erection of Harvey Court (1960-2) on West Road, some distance from the main college buildings. It was designed by Sir Leslie Martin, professor of architecture in the University.

Jesus College

The open courts set in spacious grounds, which distinguish Jesus from all the other colleges, are an inheritance from the Priory of St Radegund, founded in the 1130s. Never a very wealthy institution, by the end of the 15th century it had so declined that only two nuns were left, and one of those had a dubious reputation. The priory was abolished in 1496 by John Alcock, bishop of Ely, who founded Jesus College in its place. The visitor will notice Bishop Alcock's rebus, a cockerel standing on a globe, in many places throughout his college.

Bishop Alcock used most of the priory buildings for his new foundation. The nuns' chapel was too big for college purposes, so the north and south aisles were demolished and the nave was shortened. Today it looks more like a grand parish church than the usual college chapel (**36**), and in fact it was used as such until 1555. The rest of the priory buildings were converted into chambers for scholars. The old chapter house was demolished, but in the 19th century its beautiful arcaded 13th-century entrance was uncovered behind a wall of Cloister Court, where it can still be seen. The hall, which had been the nuns' refectory, was restored and the great oriel window inserted. The bishop also initiated some completely new building, notably the elegant gate tower which stands back from Jesus Lane, at the end of a walled walk known as the Chimney (**37**). E. M. Forster wrote that 'the Chimney, to me, is part of a delicate dramatic effect; at the end of its calculated dullness rises Alcock's rich Gate Tower, promising a different world – a promise faithfully fulfilled'.

The Cloister Court dates from the 16th century; the original simple Tudor windows of its outer walls were replaced by the present arches in the 18th century (**38**). It looks especially pretty in summer, when baskets of flowers are hung from each arch. Apart from the completion of the First Court during the 17th century with the range opposite the gate tower, few changes were made to the college during the next 150 years. In the 19th century, to cope with increasing student numbers, new accommodation was built to the design of Sir Alfred Waterhouse, in bright red brick. Restoration of the chapel was undertaken, initially by Pugin. Stained glass windows, designed by the pre-Raphaelite artist Sir Edward Burne-Jones, were installed and the ceiling of the nave was painted with designs by William Morris. (All Saints' Church in Jesus Lane also has lavish interior decoration by these artists.) The 19th- and early-20th-century architecture of Jesus College perhaps suffers from over-conscious imitation of the existing medieval buildings. The modern North Court (erected 1963-5) is far more adventurous (**39**).

The many distinguished men who studied at Jesus include Thomas Cranmer

OVERLEAF ►

37 (left) *Jesus College: the 15th-century gate tower built by the college's founder, Bishop Alcock, and the approach to it, known as The Chimney*

38 (right) *Jesus College cloister evokes the early history of the college as a convent; the lawn of the First Court is reflected in the near lantern*

▲ **39** *Modern undergraduate accommodation in Jesus College designed by David Roberts, a local architect*

(1489-1556), the archbishop of Canterbury martyred by Mary Tudor; Fulke Greville (1554-1628), poet and friend of Sir Philip Sidney; Laurence Sterne (1713-68), author of *Tristram Shandy;* and Samuel Taylor Coleridge (1772-1834), who had an eventful undergraduate career, absconding from college to join the 15th Dragoons under the name of Silas Tomkins Comberbacke. He returned to Cambridge, but a combination of debt and unorthodox opinions obliged him to leave again. Later in life he often recalled nostalgically how 'in an inauspicious hour I left the friendly cloisters and happy grove of quiet, ever-honoured Jesus College'. Notable 20th-century alumni include Jacob Bronowski, the Earl of Snowdon and Alistair Cooke.

King's College

King's College Chapel (**41**, **42**) is deservedly the best-known building in Cambridge. The exterior has been painted by Turner and the interior by Canaletto. Wordsworth wrote three sonnets on it; more recently it has been the subject of a poem by John Betjeman. Saint-Saëns admired the singing of the choir, which in the 20th century has become world famous through the annual broadcast of the service of nine lessons and carols on Christmas Eve.

The chapel is all that was realised of Henry VI's ambitious scheme for a new college. Soon after the construction (1441) of the modest Old Court (sold to the University in 1829 and now part of the Old Schools), the king decided that his new foundation should be much grander than originally intended, and instigated the purchase and clearance of a large site between the High Street (now

King's Parade) and the river. The new college was a dual foundation with Eton College, from which it took its scholars, on the model of William of Wykeham's New College, Oxford, which was linked to Winchester College.

Henry's plans included a huge chapel joined to an arcaded court, a lofty bell tower and a cloistered cemetery court by the river. Building delays were caused not only by lack of money but by civil unrest culminating in the Wars of the Roses, in which Henry eventually lost his crown. The chapel was begun on 25 July 1446, when the king himself laid the foundation stone; building stopped in 1461 when he was deposed. Outside the west end one can see how much had been built: the original white limestone stops abruptly 2 – 2½ m above ground level (the east end had progressed further). Work continued, with many interruptions, under Henry's successors, Edward IV, Richard III and Henry VII, who all provided money for the completion of the college. Henry VII's architect, John Wastell of Bury St Edmunds, was probably largely responsible for the fan vaulting (he also designed the similar smaller-scale fan vaulting in the retrochoir at Peterborough Cathedral). The fittings, including the screen and the stained glass windows, were financed by Henry VIII. The chapel was finished by 1536, 90 years after Henry VI founded it, and no more of his scheme was ever built; yet he had signally affected the development of Cambridge. The vastness of his plan almost certainly influenced the scale of the later foundations of Trinity and St John's, and the clearance of land by the river was the beginning of the Backs.

▼ **40** *King's College choristers on their way to a service, wearing their traditional Eton collars and top hats*

◄ **41** *King's College*
Chapel: the interior of the
inner chapel, looking east

The chapel is almost drily simple in plan, but this austerity is belied by the richness of its interior decoration (**41**). The varied heraldic carvings below the windows at the west end, an addition by the Tudor monarchs who completed the chapel, include their emblems of the rose and portcullis. The visitor needs no guide to the beauty of the fan vaulting – the largest, simplest and grandest of the many vaults in this style. (The smaller, more elaborate vaulting at Henry VII's Chapel at Westminster Abbey and St George's Chapel, Windsor, make interesting comparisons.) Yet this 'branching roof' (Wordsworth) serves no structural purpose: the real roof is supported on a timber frame.

It is exceptionally fortunate that the original glass should have survived in a building which gives such architectural emphasis to the windows – an especially valuable survival in England, which lost almost all its medieval glass in the Reformation and the Protectorate. No one knows why the glass here was spared. The original glass remains in 25 of the windows, only the west window and the upper half of the window to the right of the altar being modern additions. The Flemish designers (the names of most of them are recorded) drew on Renaissance, not medieval, artistic styles, and were perhaps influenced by Raphael's tapestry cartoons. The windows should be looked at in order, beginning at the north-west corner and working east. Most of them share the same iconographical scheme: the bottom half of each has two scenes from the New Testament and the top half has the scenes from the Old Testament which, according to contemporary theology, prefigured the events depicted below. In the middle of each window stand 'messenger' figures who carry scrolls bearing the appropriate biblical text. (A pair of binoculars helps to identify the many details not readily visible to the naked eye.)

The large carved oak organ screen was financed by Henry VIII. It can be dated to 1533-6, for it bears the arms and initials of Henry's ill-fated second wife, Anne Boleyn, as well as the king's own monogram. This is the first major example in England of Italianate Renaissance wood carving and is of the very highest quality, but the identity and even the nationality of the men who created it remain unknown. The sumptuous stalls are mainly contemporary with it; the canopies are 17th-century additions. The east end of the chapel was remodelled in the 1960s to accommodate the gift to the college of Rubens' *The Adoration of the Magi*, at that time the most expensive painting ever sold at auction. Victorian panelling was removed, the inner chapel repaved to its original 18th-century design and the painting placed over the altar.

Henry VI's great court was not finished until 300 years after completion of the chapel. In 1713 the provost (the college's name for its master) employed Hawksmoor, Wren's greatest pupil, to design new buildings. Hawksmoor followed Henry VI's groundplan closely but his proposed new court was in the Palladian, not the Gothic, style. In his original plans Henry had specified that the college buildings should be grand but plain, without excessive ornament. Though his intention was ignored by the Tudors in their completion of the chapel, it was observed 200 years later when the provost told Hawksmoor he 'desir'd all ornaments might be avoided . . . because something of that Nature is in the Founder's will'. However, building was delayed and the court that was eventually begun in 1724 was designed by James Gibbs, the architect of the Senate House. Only one side was constructed – the Fellows' Building, whose uncompromisingly 18th-century style nevertheless blends happily with the chapel to create from the Backs one of the most famous views in England (**42**).

Plans for completing the court were put forward by Robert Adam in 1784, but nothing was done until 1824, when the architect was William Wilkins. His design, if slightly too symmetrical for modern tastes, manages to complement the chapel without competing with it (**43**); fortunately his plan to 'Gothicise' Gibbs' Fellows' Building was never implemented. The founder's statue (1879) dominates the immaculate lawn.

The college changed greatly during the 19th century. In 1851 it abandoned its old privilege of claiming degrees for its students without their taking any University examination. In 1873 non-Etonians were at last admitted to scholarships and the first non-Etonian fellow was elected. King's had already had some notable members. The great composer Orlando Gibbons sang in its choir at the end of the 16th century. The 17th-century poet Edmund Waller studied here, as did the 18th-century writer Horace Walpole, son of England's first Prime Minister and pioneer of the Romantic taste for Gothic. King's was noted for intellectual brilliance at the turn of the 19th and 20th centuries and subsequently under the provostship of M. R. James, the great medievalist now best remembered for his ghost stories (some of which are set in Cambridge). The novelist E. M. Forster was an undergraduate and later honorary fellow, and describes college life in *The Longest Journey* and *Maurice*. The eminent economist Maynard Keynes, having studied at King's, eventually became college bursar. The college library contains many manuscripts of the poet Rupert Brooke, who had a dazzling undergraduate career. More recent students include the Nobel Prize-winning novelist Patrick White.

▲ **42** *A view of King's College Backs in early spring; to the right of the chapel is Gibbs' Fellows' Building and to the left is Clare College Old Court*

▶ **43** *The frontage of King's College on King's Parade; the gateway was built in the early 19th century. A Victorian pillar box stands outside*

48

Magdalene College

44 *Magdalene College: above the doorway in the First Court leading to the hall and to the Pepys Building is the coat of arms of the college's founder, Lord Audley, carved in the 17th century*

Like many other colleges dating from the second major series of foundations, Magdalene (pronounced 'maudlin') incorporates the buildings of an earlier, religious establishment – in this case Monks' Hostel, a Benedictine educational institution. It was also known as Buckingham College because of the large benefactions it received from late-15th-century Dukes of Buckingham, who built the chapel and hall. At the dissolution of the monasteries the hostel passed to Thomas, Lord Audley, the Lord Chancellor of England, who in 1542 founded the present college. Magdalene is unusual in that its master is not elected by the fellows but chosen by the heirs of Lord Audley of Audley End, the great Jacobean mansion near Saffron Walden; it is also the only ancient college situated on the west bank of the Cam.

The First Court, of beautiful red brick (**44**), was erected piecemeal in the 15th and 16th centuries. The elaborate gallery and double staircase were inserted in the hall in 1714. The splendid silver sconces here are not merely decorative, for the hall is still lit only by candles. Attempts to raise money for a new building in the 1640s bore fruit soon after 1660 in the Pepys Building, which has a pretty semi-classical façade (**45**) but from the Fellows' Garden behind looks more like a country gentleman's house. Its name and the date (1724) over the central arch of its arcade refer to the installation of the celebrated library which Samuel Pepys left to his old college. This can still be seen in its 12 original bookcases of red oak made for Pepys in 1666. The collection

45 *Magdalene College: the front of the 17th-century Pepys Building, which contains the Pepys Library*

contains many valuable manuscripts and books, but its chief treasure is the manuscript of Pepys' famous shorthand diary (first published 1825). Throughout his career as MP, secretary to the Admiralty and president of the Royal Society Pepys remembered his happy undergraduate days at Magdalene. His diary for 25 May 1668 records a visit to his old college: 'I took my boy . . . and walked to Magdalene College; and there into the butterys as a stranger, and there drank my belly full of their beer, which pleased me, as the best I ever drank: and hear by the butler's man, who was son to Goody Mulliner over-against the college that we used to buy stewed prunes of, concerning the college and persons in it; and find very few . . . that were of my time . . .'

Magdalene Street, which still has a provision shop much patronised by Magdalene undergraduates, is mostly owned by the college and contains Cambridge's best surviving examples of medieval domestic architecture. It is now a row of picturesque shops but was formerly a slum, notorious for its many brothels: in his *Tour through . . . Great Britain* Defoe was shocked that a college should be surrounded by such squalid dwellings. The redevelopment and building of student accommodation between Magdalene Street and St John's has remained small-scale and in keeping with the beautiful surroundings.

Pembroke College

In the mid 14th century the University gave Mary de St Pol, Countess of Pembroke, a small piece of land to establish a new college. The rest of Pembroke's site was acquired piecemeal and did not reach its present extent until the 16th century.

The most notable survival of the foundress's original court, now called Old Court, is the considerably restored 14th-century gateway. It is surmounted by a pair of pretty 17th-century oriel windows flanking the college coat of arms, carved in stone. The court was much enlarged in the 19th century by the removal of the south range, so that it now includes the new chapel and the attractive arcade known as Hitcham's Cloister, named after a 17th-century benefactor. The original chapel, on the north side of the court, was completely remodelled after the building of the new chapel (1690) and until the 19th century was used as a library; it has a superb plasterwork ceiling.

The present chapel (**46**) is of great interest as the first completed work by Sir Christopher Wren. In 1659 his uncle Matthew Wren, bishop of Ely and fellow of Pembroke, was released from the Tower of London after 17 years' imprisonment, and determined to provide his college with a new chapel as a thanksgiving. He asked his nephew, then a professor at Oxford, to design it. The new chapel (consecrated 1665) was the most purely classical building that Cambridge had yet seen. For the first time an architect showed sensitivity in designing the street front of a college building: the west end of the chapel, on Trumpington Street, is most harmonious. The interior has a very ornate plaster ceiling.

A new court was built beyond the hall in the 17th century. The north range was constructed between 1614 and 1616 and Hitcham's Building opposite was begun in 1655. The gate in the wall beyond (**47**), which forms the entrance to the extensive and beautiful garden, is the stone door-case (1634) removed from the entrance to the old hall in 1878. The old hall was demolished in the 19th century on the advice of the architect Waterhouse, who thought it likely to

◄46 Pembroke College Chapel, Sir Christopher Wren's first building

53

collapse at any moment; in fact it took several charges of dynamite to bring it down. Waterhouse then rebuilt the hall and added buildings beyond the chapel in the style of a Loire château. Pembroke is more fortunate than either Gonville and Caius or Balliol College, Oxford, where Waterhouse also built, in that its grounds are sufficiently extensive to absorb the architect's new buildings and prevent them from overshadowing the older parts of the college. None the less, it is difficult to like an architect who wished to add a huge campanile to Wren's chapel 'high enough to be the most conspicuous tower in Cambridge'.

The list of famous men who studied at Pembroke is longer than that of many larger colleges. Nicholas Ridley, the great church reformer who is thought to have helped Cranmer with the new Protestant prayer book, was made a fellow in *c.* 1524. In prison shortly before his martyrdom in 1555 he wrote a moving letter of farewell in which he remembers his time at Pembroke: 'Farewell therefore Cambridge, my loving mother and tender nurse . . . Farewell Pembroke Hall, of late mine own college, my care and my charge . . . in thy orchard (the walls . . . and trees, if they could speak, would bear me witness) I learned without book almost all Paul's Epistles . . . the sweet smell thereof I trust I shall carry with me into heaven . . .' Pembroke also fostered the studies of several famous poets: Edmund Spenser, author of *The Faerie Queene* and a favourite of Elizabeth I; Thomas Gray (author of the 'Elegy in a Country Churchyard') who found tranquillity here after his torment at Peterhouse; and the brilliant but unstable Christopher Smart. In 1773 William Pitt entered the college, aged 15; he left in 1780 and within three years he was Prime Minister.

▲ **47** *Pembroke College: the gateway to the garden, which was originally at the entrance to the college's old dining hall*

► **48** *Peterhouse: the dining hall, which dates back to the 13th century*

Peterhouse

The oldest college in Cambridge is properly 'St Peter's', but for centuries it has been known as Peterhouse. In 1280 Hugh of Balsham established a community of scholars at St John's Hospital, following the example set by Walter de Merton at the new Merton College, Oxford. In 1284 the scholars moved to the present site, some hostels then outside the Trumpington Gate. Money bequeathed by Hugh of Balsham was used to build the hall, the oldest surviving college building in Cambridge (**48**). It has been considerably altered, and in the 19th century was decorated by the firm of William Morris.

►50 Peterhouse: the 18th-century Fellows' Building, designed by Sir James Burrough

There was no need to build a chapel straight away, for the scholars could use the Church of St Peter's-without-Trumpington-Gate, which since its rebuilding (1340-52) has been known as Little St Mary's. It is still connected by a gallery to Peterhouse. American visitors may be particularly interested in its memorial (on the north wall) to the Rev. Godfrey Washington, a fellow of Peterhouse (died 1729), bearing the Washington coat of arms – traditionally the origin of the stars and stripes of the American flag. The graveyard, a romantic tangle of graves and trees and flowers, and the picturesque cottages of Little St Mary's Lane, together make one of the loveliest corners of Cambridge.

The rest of the main court was erected in the 15th century, and like many other college courts was given a classical façade in the 18th century. Its dullness is relieved in summer by boxes of bright red geraniums on the window sills. The chapel (1628-32), unusually positioned in the middle of the open side of the court (**49**), is a delightful example of the English Baroque style, largely inspired by the high-church revival under Charles I. It suffered badly at the hands of the Puritans, but fortunately the great east window, erected in 1630 and made to a

*▼49 Peterhouse Chapel (17th century): its position, in the centre of an open side of the main court, was later imitated by Wren at Emmanuel (**33**)*

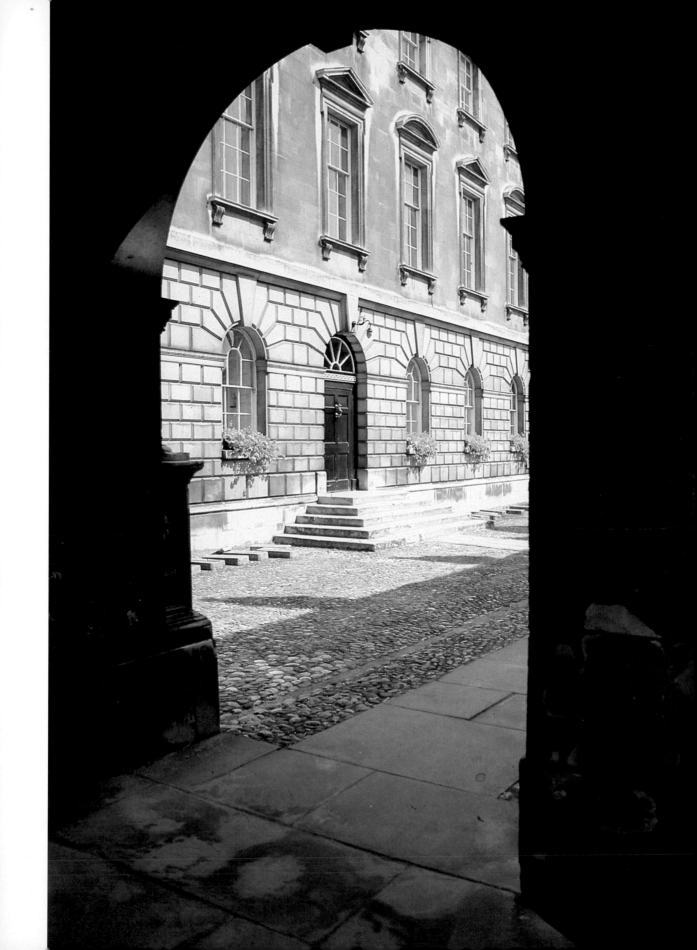

design of Rubens, was removed in time and hidden until the Restoration of Charles II. The rest of the glass was installed in the 19th century: it is quite exceptionally horrible. In 1738 the new building designed by Burrough (**50**) was erected parallel to the chapel. It completes the varied and very attractive frontage of Peterhouse onto Trumpington Street. Opposite is a fine 18th-century town house built (1702) by Dr Charles Beaumont, who died in 1726, leaving his house to the college to be used as the Master's Lodge.

The poet Thomas Gray was at Peterhouse from 1734 to 1738; he returned in 1743 but left for good in 1756 in unfortunate circumstances. Being terrified of fire, he kept a rope in his room as a means of escape. This much amused a group of undergraduates who spent more time hunting than studying, and they decided to hunt Gray by shouting 'fire!' under his window. Gray did not jump out, but he was so upset that he changed his college for Pembroke, across the road. The iron bars he placed across the window, to which he could attach his rope, still exist in his rooms in the Fellows' Building.

Queens' College

The early history of Queens' resembles that of Christ's, in that a small and poor foundation was taken over and refurbished by an aristocratic lady with a zeal for education. St Bernard's College was founded in 1446 by Andrew Dockett, rector of St Botolph's, on the site of an old priory. Within a year Queen Margaret of Anjou (wife to Henry VI (the founder of King's College), gained her husband's consent to refound and rename St Bernard's. She thought that this would lead to 'laud and honneure of sexe femnine' and that the absence of a Cambridge college founded by a queen of England was a grievous omission. The foundation stone of Queen Margaret's College was laid in 1448. Fortunately after Henry's deposition Queen Elizabeth, wife of his enemy Edward IV, decided to continue her predecessor's work. She granted the college its statutes and finished its buildings. Queens' College regards itself as having been founded by both queens; hence the apostrophe *after* the s in the college's name.

The First Court of Queens' can well claim to be the prettiest of Cambridge's smaller courts; it certainly gives the best impression of what a late medieval college looked like. Its mellow red brick has survived so well that the court has remained virtually unrenovated. The architect (probably Reginald of Ely) included in the east side a splendid gate tower, one of the many in Cambridge designed to protect the colleges' treasuries. The mid-17th-century sundial on the north wall (**51**) was renewed in 1733. The buildings by the river were begun soon after the completion of the First Court, to which they are linked by the highly picturesque timber and plaster gallery (**52**) of the President's Lodge (Queens' has a president rather than a master). The quaint cloister below – Cambridge's only medieval cloister – was continued around three sides of this utterly delightful court, which forms an ideal setting for Queens' Drama Society's performances of Shakespeare every May Week.

The lavishly painted hall, a basically 16th-century structure, was (like most college halls) altered in the 18th century when classical architecture was fashionable and Gothic despised, and promptly altered again in the 19th century when the reverse obtained. Many of the Victorian alterations and decorations were, like those at Peterhouse, made by the firm of William Morris. The tower in the south-west corner of Old Court is traditionally known as

◄ 51 Queens' College: the 15th-century First Court, with its 17th-century sundial

▲ **53** *Queens' College Mathematical Bridge: a copy of the original of 1749-50*

Erasmus' Tower; the great humanist scholar lived in Queens' (1511-14) whilst teaching as Lady Margaret Reader in Greek and Professor of Divinity in the University. Though he complained about the cold damp Cambridge weather and the 'raw, small and windy' college ale, he later looked back on the University's hospitality with some affection.

James Essex designed all that was built (1756-60) of a larger scheme for rebuilding the whole river front, never carried out. The medieval buildings are enhanced by the famous timber Mathematical Bridge (**53**). The present structure (1902) is a copy of the original constructed in 1749-50. Further building took place in the 19th and 20th centuries. Sir Basil Spence's new building (1959) caused a sensation, so shocked was Cambridge at the idea of a modern building on the Backs. It now looks tame and fiddly; Powell and Moya's Cripps Building is bolder and better.

St Catharine's College

The college takes its name and crest (a wheel) from the mythical St Catharine of Alexandria, a patroness of learning, whose sanctity was such that it caused the wheel on which she was about to be martyred to break into pieces.

◄ **52** *Queens' College: the President's Lodge, a beautiful example of early-16th-century domestic architecture*

Robert Woodlark, third provost of King's, founded St Catharine's in 1473 as a small society of priests who would spend their time praying for their founder's soul and studying theology and philosophy. The study of non-religious subjects

▲ 54 *St Catharine's College: the main court on Trumpington Street was begun in the 17th century*

– medicine and law – was expressly forbidden. At first there were no under-graduate members, although by this time the concept of a college as a teaching institution as well as a home for scholars was widely accepted. However, by the 16th century the college was obliged – probably to increase its income – to become a teaching body.

Initially the main entrance was on Queens' Lane; the rest of the college was separated from Trumpington Street by a row of houses. Its buildings, never very splendid, were so dilapidated by the 17th century that it was decided, as at Clare, to rebuild completely. The main court (**54**) was begun in 1673. The chapel was finished in 1704; it contains extremely fine contemporary wood-work. James Essex designed a new building for the south-east side of the court (1757-72); the north side was 'Gothicised' in the 19th century to harmonise with the oriel window added to the old hall. By now the college had acquired the land alongside Trumpington Street and demolished the houses there. It was origin-ally intended that a fourth, eastern side should be added to the court, but this was never constructed and the court remains three-sided, in the Cambridge tradition begun by John Caius in the 16th century. The buildings of St Catharine's, much admired by John Ruskin, are in a dark-coloured brick that makes them look rather gaunt except in bright sunshine; a fourth side would have plunged the whole court into permanent gloom.

John Addenbrooke, founder of Addenbrooke's Hospital, entered St Catharine's in 1697. By then the founder's restrictions on subjects of study had been forgotten, and Addenbrooke graduated MD in 1711. In his will he left his medicine chest to his old college, which still owns it. Other well-known students at St Catharine's have included the dramatist James Shirley (1596-1666) and the novelist Malcolm Lowry (1909-57). One of the youngest Cambridge under-graduates ever admitted was William Wotton (born 1666), who knew Hebrew, Greek and Latin by the time he was six and entered St Catharine's at the age of nine. At 21 he became a fellow of the Royal Society, but his later career was undistinguished.

In 1880, when the fortunes of St Catharine's were at a low ebb, it was suggested that the college be merged with King's. The idea did not receive enough support to be carried out, but memories of it were revived between 1965 and 1968 when St Catharine's and King's co-operated in the rebuilding of King's Lane, which runs between the two colleges. The development includes a new hall for St Catharine's; the old hall became the Senior Combination (= Common) Room.

St John's College

55 St John's College: the 18th-century Old Bridge, built by Robert Grumbold, Wren's master mason for Trinity Library and son of the designer of Clare Bridge

Like Christ's College, St John's is the creation of Lady Margaret Beaufort, Henry VII's mother. She never saw her new college, for she died before its foundation in 1511; it was brought into being by her friend John Fisher, bishop of Rochester, who chose for it the site of the 13th-century Hospital of St John. The First Court incorporated the old chapel of the hospital. The gatehouse, with Lady Margaret's coat of arms over the entrance, survives in its original state. Its elegant proportions contrast well with Trinity's massive Great Gate, and it is often reckoned to be the most beautiful of Cambridge's gatehouses.

◄ **56** *St John's College:
the gateway from the
Second Court to the Third
Court. The lozenge of
arms belongs to the
Countess of Shrewsbury,
who financed the building
of Second Court*

St John's early years coincided with Erasmus' introduction of humanist scholarship to Cambridge, and the college soon established itself as an important centre of learning. Its teachers included Roger Ascham, who assisted in the spread of the new European ideas and later became Queen Elizabeth's tutor, and among his students was Thomas Wyatt, the first poet to introduce Italian forms into English literature. The college also expanded rapidly, and for long was the largest in the University.

The Second Court (1602) was mainly financed by Mary, Countess of Shrewsbury, whose statue stands above the gateway in the tower at the west end of the court. This plain but impressive example of late Elizabethan brickwork contains one of the most spectacular interiors in Cambridge, the panelled Long Gallery which is now the Senior Combination (= Common) Room. The plaster ceiling, 28 m long, dates from 1600. Work on the Third Court followed almost immediately as a result of a large donation by John Williams, bishop of Lincoln and Lord Keeper of the Privy Seal. His full title explains the large initials on the river front of the library which mystify many passers-by: ILCS, i.e. Johannes Lincolniensis Custos Sigilli. With its great bay window the library looks very beautiful from the river, and is interesting as one of the earliest English examples of deliberately 'Gothic' architecture – in a sense the first Gothic 'revival' – specified by Williams because he thought it appropriate to a library building. The rest of the small but very pretty Third Court was finished later in the 17th century.

In 1698 the college consulted Sir Christopher Wren about constructing a new bridge. This was eventually built (1708-12) by Robert Grumbold, making some use of Wren's designs (**55**); it leads to St John's spacious grounds on the far side of the river. It was here that Wordsworth liked to wander to escape from the bustle of University life. Wordsworth was at St John's from 1787 to 1790 and described his undergraduate days in his autobiographical poem *The Prelude:*

> The Evangelist St John my patron was:
> Three gloomy courts are his, and in the first
> Was my abiding place, a nook obscure;
> Right underneath, the college kitchens made
> A humming sound . . .

In 1831 St John's erected the huge New Building (**10**, **57**) on the far side of the river, at the time the largest single building of any college. It is a 19th-century dream of the Middle Ages, complete with pinnacles and cloisters in the spirit of Sir Walter Scott and Victorian Romantic operas. The whole is crowned with what can only be described as a Gothic cupola, traditionally known as the Wedding Cake. The building is linked to the Third Court by the famous picturesque 'Bridge of Sighs' (**59**), which resembles the Bridge of Sighs in Venice only in being a covered bridge. In contrast to the New Building the Victorian chapel (completed 1869) is academically correct and respectably dull. It does not harmonise with the rest of First Court, but it is happily positioned (by chance rather than design) to create some attractive views, especially from the river. The college's 1930s buildings are best unmentioned. However, its Cripps Building, designed by Powell and Moya (completed 1967) and tucked away behind the New Building, is often thought to be the finest 20th-century college building in Cambridge (**58**).

◄ **57** *St John's 19th-century New Building, seen from the river*

◄ **58** *St John's College: the Cripps Building (completed 1967), containing undergraduate accommodation*

► **59** *St John's College: the Bridge of Sighs in the setting sun, seen from a window in Third Court*

Sidney Sussex College

Sidney Sussex was the last Cambridge college to be founded until the establishment of Downing in 1800. It was built on the site of a 13th-century friary which had been suppressed in 1538, the stones being used in the construction of Henry VIII's new foundation, Trinity College. In 1589 Lady Frances Sidney, Countess of Sussex, bequeathed two-fifths of her estate to found a new college. The site was eventually acquired, after strong resistance from its owners, Trinity College, in 1594, and the first stone was laid a year later; the architect was Ralph Simons.

Most of the original buildings still survive, but were refaced by Sir Jeffry Wyatville in the early 19th century. No one has ever much liked his work, but he succeeded ingeniously in making two regular courts and a gateway out of a rather random group of buildings. Sidney's 'Tudor' turrets and battlements are a typical product of the Romantic vogue for medieval life and architecture (**60**).

In 1616 Oliver Cromwell entered the college, leaving a year later on the death of his father. Sidney Sussex did not, however, display any Parliamentarian sympathies as a result of his brief membership; when Civil War broke out the college sent £100 to the king, and Dr Ward, the master, was imprisoned for his refusal to make any contribution to the Parliamentarian cause. In 1960 the college was given a macabre relic of its most famous student in the form of Cromwell's head. This had been removed from his body when Charles II ordered that the bodies of leading Parliamentarians be dug up and destroyed. The head was buried in the chapel, in conditions of great secrecy, and only a few people know its location.

▼ **60** *Chapel Court, Sidney Sussex College. The architect of Sidney's Tudor-revival buildings, Sir Jeffry Wyatville, is best remembered today for his Romantic embellishments to Windsor Castle for George IV*

▲ **61** *The dining hall and
central fountain in Trinity
Great Court, laid out at
the end of the 16th century
by Thomas Nevile, master
of the college. To the right
of the hall is the Senior
Combination Room*

Trinity College

Its combination of intellectual distinction, architectural splendour and immense wealth gives Trinity pre-eminence amongst the colleges of Cambridge. In 1546 Henry VIII united two existing colleges, Michaelhouse (founded 1323) and King's Hall (founded by Edward III in 1336) to create a new college that would rival Christ Church, Oxford, founded by his now discredited Chancellor, Wolsey. At this date the college possessed only two buildings worthy of such aspirations: the present clock tower, with its statue of Edward III, erected between 1426 and 1437 (the first of Cambridge's many gatehouses), and Great Gate, through which the visitor enters the college from Trinity Street. Completed in 1533, this was built to the orders of Henry VIII and bears his statue over the entrance.

The present grandeur of the college is due almost entirely to its late-16th-century master Thomas Nevile, a favourite of Elizabeth I and a very rich man. Largely at his own expense he cleared what is now Great Court of a muddle of buildings and moved the clock tower to its present position at the west end of the chapel (built in the previous reign by Queen Mary). He then erected, for the sake of symmetry – though nothing in Great Court is straight or symmetrical – a tower on the opposite side of the court, bearing a statue of Elizabeth I. (On an adjoining staircase lived HRH the Prince of Wales, son of Elizabeth II, whilst an undergraduate at Trinity.) Nevile also built the hall, the largest in Cambridge (**61**, **73**), and the splendid fountain which formerly supplied the college with its drinking water and remains the focal point of this huge court – the largest court in Cambridge and larger than any at Oxford.

Beyond the hall Nevile constructed a new court (now named after him) with an elegant semi-classical cloister (**62**). Initially open to the river, it was enclosed by the addition of a new library (1676-95), designed by Sir Christopher Wren and now called the Wren Library: this is one of his finest works and one of the great buildings of Cambridge (**11, 63**). Originally it was to be circular, but in its final form it owes much to the inspiration of Sansovino's famous library in Venice. From the outside it is difficult to realise its monumental size because the exterior is so devised as not to overpower the restrained proportions of Nevile's buildings. Wren placed the floor of the library not above the arches (as it appears from the outside) but below them, filling in the tops of the arches with carved lunettes to disguise this fact – as he himself explained, to give 'the appearance of arches as the order required fair and lofty'. This trick has given the library a very spacious and well-lit interior (**64**). Wren took great trouble over its fittings, even designing the stools and revolving reading tables himself. The lavish carving in limewood which decorates the bookcases is by Grinling Gibbons, and there is a fine series of busts by Roubiliac at the bookcase ends. Treasures from the library usually on display include splendid illuminated manuscripts, a large series of early editions of Shakespeare, autograph drafts of Milton's early poems, Newton's domestic accounts and the manuscript of *Winnie the Pooh*.

Further 17th-century building was in a very different idiom: Bishop's Hostel, on the left of the entrance from Trinity Lane, is a charmingly domestic and uncollegiate-looking structure. The elegant 18th-century bridge, designed by James Essex, was incorporated in an avenue of lime trees that leads to William Wilkins' New Court in the early-19th-century Gothic style. In his poem *In*

▼**62** *Nevile's Court, Trinity College: the cloisters*

▲ 63 *The Wren Library,*
Trinity College

Memoriam Tennyson recalls walking down this avenue to revisit the rooms in which his friend Hallam had lived when they were both undergraduates at Trinity. The ante-chapel contains statues and other memorials commemorating some of Trinity's famous students. Outstanding is Roubiliac's superb statue of the great scientist Sir Isaac Newton, who spent his academic life at Trinity (1661-96). There are also statues of Sir Francis Bacon, Macaulay and Tennyson. More recent names occur on the brass wall-plaques: the philosophers A. N. Whitehead, Bertrand Russell and Ludwig Wittgenstein, and many eminent scientists (for Trinity boasts over 20 Nobel Prize winners – more than the total produced by many entire countries). A number of famous poets also studied at Trinity, including Dryden, Herbert and Marvell, but the most famous of them must be Byron. His statue (rejected by Westminster Abbey) stands in the library, perhaps rather inappropriately for a man who was known at Cambridge for keeping a bear in his rooms rather than for his academic pursuits.

Trinity Hall

Trinity Hall's name is likely to confuse the visitor. Many of the first Cambridge colleges were called halls. 'College' meant the people who lived in the hall. Soon the word acquired its modern meaning (without entirely losing its old one) and became indistinguishable from the word 'hall'. By the 19th century most of the old halls, such as Pembroke Hall and St Catharine's Hall, had adopted the name 'college', but this was impossible for Trinity Hall because a Trinity College already existed. Thus, uniquely amongst the colleges of Cambridge, it retains its old name.

◄ **64** *Trinity College: the interior of the Wren Library. The statue of Byron at the far end is by the Danish sculptor Thorwaldsen (1768-1844)*

Trinity Hall is not only entirely distinct from Trinity College; it is also much older. It was founded in 1350 by William Bateman, bishop of Norwich and church diplomatist, who intended his new institution to provide men learned in canon law for the service of the church. For over 600 years the college has maintained a tradition of legal study and produced an impressive number of judges and other eminent lawyers.

The visitor enters the college from Trinity Lane through the arch in a building erected in 1852 to replace one lost in a fire. The main court (**65**) is 14th-century but, like many others in Cambridge, was given its present well-proportioned classical appearance by refacing in the 18th century. Some idea of how the medieval buildings looked can be obtained by going through the passage beside B staircase; the wall immediately behind retains its medieval masonry and some early windows. The hall was given its present regular appearance in the 18th century, as was the chapel, which is the earliest chapel especially projected for college use, and the smallest college chapel in Cambridge. Beyond the screens on the right is the library, a very pretty piece of Elizabethan brickwork. The upper floor is preserved in its original state with chained books attached to Jacobean bookcases (**66**). The small door high up in the wall was originally at the end of a walk on top of a wall that led from the Master's Lodge opposite. The old lodge no longer exists and the wall has disappeared. The herbaceous border beside the library is especially magnificent in late summer (**67**). The gardens lead down to a terrace beside the river. Beyond the Master's Lodge is the Fellows' Garden, which is not usually open to the public, but can be easily seen through the wrought iron gate. It contains a

▼ **65** *Trinity Hall: Front Court. As in several other college courts, the early structure (14th century) was refaced in the 18th century*

number of ancient chestnut trees and another splendid herbaceous border. In 1905 the novelist Henry James wrote, 'If I were called upon . . . to mention the prettiest corner of the world I should draw out a thoughtful sigh and point the way to the garden of Trinity Hall.'

Not all the eminent men who have studied at the college are part of its legal tradition. Robert Herrick, the 17th-century author of the well-known lyric 'Gather ye rosebuds while ye may', studied here. In the 18th century Trinity Hall undergraduates included Viscount Fitzwilliam, founder of the Fitzwilliam Museum, and Lord Chesterfield, author of a famous series of letters to his son about how to do well in society which Dr Johnson condemned as teaching 'the morals of a whore and the manners of a dancing master'. More recent names include the Victorian man of letters Sir Leslie Stephen and the novelists Bulwer-Lytton, Ronald Firbank and J. B. Priestley.

19th- and 20th-century colleges

The founding of colleges in late-19th-century Cambridge was usually prompted by one of two motives: the furtherance of Christian religion and the cause of university education for women.

The abolition (1871) of the statute requiring all prospective fellows of colleges and professors to give evidence that they were practising members of the Church of England caused some fears that religious influence in Cambridge life would be dangerously diminished, and was partly responsible for the foundation (1882) of a new college on Church of England principles for the education of men of moderate means. It was named **Selwyn College** in memory of George Selwyn, one of the first bishops of New Zealand, later bishop of Lichfield, and was modelled on Keble College, Oxford, with the intention of combining 'sober living and high culture of the mind . . . with Christian training'. It achieved full collegiate status in 1958. The first buildings (1879-81), in a Tudor Gothic style, are by Sir Arthur Blomfield (**71**). The college retains strong links with the Church of England; its statutes require the master to be a clerk in holy orders.

Concurrently several theological colleges were founded in Cambridge to provide better-educated clergymen. Their students are not members of the University, though they can take some of its examinations, including the theological tripos. **Westminster College** was founded in 1844 to train Presbyterian ministers; it moved to its Cambridge site at the base of Castle Hill in 1892. Designed by H. T. Hare, it is architecturally probably the most interesting of the theological colleges. In 1881 two Anglican colleges were founded, **Ridley Hall** and **Westcott House**. Opposite the latter in Jesus Lane is the Methodist **Wesley House** (founded 1921). **St Edmund's House**, on Mt Pleasant, was founded in 1896 to educate Catholic priests; in 1965, while retaining a predominantly Catholic character, it became a graduate college of the University.

The acrimonious debate about the education of women at Cambridge lasted nearly 100 years and is one of the worst blots on the University's history. In 1867 Emily Davies, a seasoned champion of women's education, began to raise money to establish a women's college. Victorian society was shocked by the idea of giving young ladies such intellectual and social freedom, which would inevitably result (it was feared) in improper behaviour. Emily Davies, herself extremely proper, was aware of such dangers, but they did nothing to lessen her determination to give women the chance to compete on equal terms with male undergraduates. Her new college, initially at Hitchin (halfway between Cambridge and London), moved to Cambridge in 1873, to a site near Girton village about three miles from the city centre – a safe distance from the temptations of idle undergraduates. The architect of **Girton College** was Sir Alfred Waterhouse. The rather forbidding aspect of his red brick buildings (**68**) is offset by their beautiful and very extensive grounds.

In 1868 the University, which at this time favoured the cause of women's education, instituted a local examination for women over 18; it was conceived of as a qualification for governesses and schoolteachers, and preparatory courses for it were arranged by the Association for the Promotion of Higher Education for Women, under the guidance of Henry Sidgwick, a fellow of Trinity. Several scholarships were also founded, one by the philosopher J. S. Mill. It soon became clear that a residential house was needed for women studying for the examination, and in 1871 Sidgwick persuaded Ann Jemima Clough, sister of the poet Arthur Hugh Clough, to take charge of a house in Regent Street. Subsequently the new institution moved to Merton Hall (now the 'School of Pythagoras'), in the grounds of St John's, before acquiring its own site where Newnham Hall, later **Newnham College,** was opened in 1875. Building continued until 1910, to the designs of Basil Champneys, in an exceptionally attractive William and Mary style (**69**). Perhaps unfortunately for the cause of women's education, relationships between Girton and Newnham were strained. Emily Davies despised Newnham for its willingness to compromise

►**68** *The entrance to Girton College (founded 1869), the first women's college established at Cambridge; it now admits male undergraduates as well*

with University authorities and failure to appreciate her belief in the need for complete equality between her students and male undergraduates.

The first move in the bid for membership of the University by Girton and Newnham was to press for permission to allow women students to attend University lectures. Most lecturers allowed this with very little fuss (despite the story of the lecturer who persisted in addressing his audience, consisting entirely of women, as 'gentlemen'). In 1881 women were allowed to take University examinations but still were not entitled to take degrees, although London University began giving degrees to women in 1878. There was a sensation in 1890 when a woman, Philippa Fawcett, received the highest marks in the mathematical tripos, for it had long been assumed that mathematics was too intellectually testing for women. This strengthened the arguments for admitting women for degrees, but the University was becoming increasingly hostile to women's education. A ballot was finally taken in 1897, at which all Cambridge MAs were entitled to vote. The subject had raised extraordinary interest and special trains were laid on to bring intending voters from London. The streets were packed with undergraduates (who were mainly against the admission of women), banners were hung from Gonville and Caius and an effigy of a female student dressed in blue bloomers and riding a bicycle was suspended from the window of the shop opposite. Dons awaiting the result of the vote in Senate House Yard were pelted with flour, confetti and fireworks. The vote was overwhelmingly against admitting women for degrees, and there were wild celebrations in the Market Place throughout the night.

The question was not raised again for over 20 years. In 1919 Oxford, without any commotion, granted women full membership of the University, but the Royal Commission investigating the affairs of Cambridge (for now that the University received public money it fell under government scrutiny) recommended that 'Cambridge should remain mainly and predominantly a "men's

▼**69** *Newnham College, the second women's college founded at Cambridge: the attractive mainly Edwardian buildings are set in a spacious garden*

▲ 70 *New Hall, the most recently founded women's college, is dominated by its domed dining hall*

university" though of a mixed type as it is already'. Prejudice eventually died of its own accord. In 1926 women were admitted as members of University faculties and allowed to hold University teaching posts and compete for University prizes. In 1947 there was almost no protest when it was decided to admit women to full membership of the University by allowing them to take degrees. The first woman Cambridge graduate was Queen Elizabeth, wife of George VI, who in 1948 received the honorary degree of Doctor of Laws.

Homerton College, an approved college of the University for teacher training, admits men and women to study for the education tripos. Between 1873 and 1892 its buildings on Hills Road housed Cavendish College, which was founded to make university education available to those of limited means, but had to close for lack of money. In 1949 **Hughes Hall** was founded as an institute of the University to train women graduates as teachers. In 1954 a new undergraduate college for women, **New Hall,** was founded. It now inhabits virginal white buildings on the Huntingdon Road designed by Chamberlin, Powell and Bon (1962-6). The dome of its neo-Byzantine dining hall, often compared unfavourably to a peeled orange, has become a familiar landmark (**70**). In 1965 **Lucy Cavendish College,** for women whose studies have been postponed or interrupted, was recognised by the University. Despite these developments, in 1970 only 12% of all undergraduate places were open to women. Then in 1972 three men's colleges, Clare, King's and Churchill, began to admit women, and other colleges rapidly followed suit. In 1979 Girton admitted its first male undergraduates. **Robinson College** (founded by David Robinson, a Cambridge-born millionaire) admitted its first undergraduates in

1979 and is especially notable as the first undergraduate Cambridge college to have been founded for both men and women. The building (opened 1980) was designed by Gillespie, Kidd and Coia as a single brick block which looks onto extensive gardens (**75**). The chapel contains stained glass by John Piper.

Concurrently with the early battles for women's education, the University concerned itself with the problem of potential students too poor to pay for college residence, and in 1869 it founded a special non-collegiate institution to enable them to study at Cambridge. In 1887 the institution bought houses in Trumpington Street and began to establish some corporate identity, assuming the name of Fitzwilliam House because of its location opposite the Fitzwilliam Museum. After World War II attempts were made to give it collegiate status and in 1964 **Fitzwilliam College** was established in new buildings on the Huntingdon Road beyond New Hall. The architect, Denys Lasdun, employed a snail-shell pattern with the hall at the centre and the residential blocks uncoiling outwards as money becomes available for further building. The hall is the most notable feature: it is finely proportioned with great clerestory windows rising to an elegant roof lantern that looks as though it is made of spun sugar.

Churchill College (founded 1960) is intended as the national monument to Sir Winston Churchill. Most of its undergraduates study scientific subjects. The buildings, a series of open courtyards better suited to a Mediterranean climate than to the piercing winds of East Anglia, were designed by Richard Sheppard (**72**). Far from the rest of the college is the chapel, erected in 1967 after considerable controversy – many of the fellows thinking a chapel completely out of place in a college whose studies were chiefly scientific. The library contains a large archive of Churchill family papers and a tapestry by Jean Lurçat presented

▼ **71** *The architect of Selwyn's innocuous Tudor buildings was Arthur Blomfield, one of whose pupils was Thomas Hardy. He was a busy and popular architect, responsible for much restoration and rebuilding at Trinity and Emmanuel Colleges; he was knighted in 1889, the year Selwyn was completed*

by General de Gaulle. In the grounds there are sculptures by Henry Moore and
Barbara Hepworth.

The graduate population of Cambridge has grown enormously since World
War II. Initially graduates who came from other universities to do research at
Cambridge lacked accommodation and social facilities. In 1965 the University
founded its own college for graduates. The buildings in Barton Road were
erected largely at the expense of the Wolfson Foundation, and hence the name
of the new college was changed from University College to **Wolfson College.**
The graduate college most likely to be noticed by visitors to Cambridge is
Darwin College (1964) on Silver Street, by the river. It consists of George
Darwin's old family home Newnham Grange and a neighbouring house, The
Hermitage. The modern extensions by Howell, Killick, Partridge and Amis
(the architects of the University's Graduate Centre on the opposite bank of the
river), which include an octagonal dining hall on stilts, blend well with the old
houses.

In 1965 Clare College together with benefactors from the USA founded an
independent graduate college, **Clare Hall.** The architect, Ralph Erskine,
completely broke with traditional concepts of college building by providing a
domestic arrangement of flats, houses and walkways surrounded by gardens, as
a setting for academic family life.

4 Life in the Modern University

The organisation of the University today is complex and seems confusing. The links between the colleges and the University are surprisingly informal. In no sense are the colleges administered by the University, although they are in effect subject to it. The University is the examining and degree giving body, but the colleges' formal obligations do not go much beyond a duty to contribute to the University's income (in proportion to their wealth) and to reserve a quota of fellowships for professors. The University and the individual colleges have separate statutes, which can be changed only by agreement with the Privy Council. In practice the most important link between University and colleges is the fact that nearly all lecturers and professors hold college fellowships, and most fellows (elected senior members of colleges, known as dons) also have University teaching posts such as lectureships or professorships. These posts are connected to faculties or departments of the University, each concerned with its own subject – history, mathematics or medicine, for instance; the faculties are responsible for the organisation of the curriculum and the setting of examinations, and lectures are given in their buildings.

The head of the University is the Chancellor. Usually a prominent politician or a member of the Royal Family (the Duke of Edinburgh was elected Chancellor in 1976), he is essentially a ceremonial figurehead but he comes to Cambridge at least once a year, if only to present honorary degrees to eminent people whom the University has decided to honour. This is the occasion of a splendid ceremony, when the Chancellor in his robes processes around Senate House Yard, led by the Esquire Bedells – ceremonial officials carrying the University maces – and followed by the candidates for degrees wearing scarlet gowns.

The real head of the University government is the Vice-Chancellor, who is elected every two years from amongst the heads of all the colleges. The Vice-Chancellor has a 'cabinet', the Council of the Senate, but in practice the most influential body is the General Board of the Faculties, which controls teaching and research. The University's legislature is theoretically the total number of its MAs (Masters of Arts); and at Cambridge an MA degree is awarded automatically on payment of a fee three years after graduation as BA (Bachelor of Arts). All living MAs are 'members of the senate' and entitled to vote on matters of general concern; but these are rare, and nowadays are usually restricted to the election of the Chancellor. Real power is vested in the Regent House, composed of MAs resident in Cambridge who are the heads or fellows of colleges or University academic and administrative staff. If any proposed decision (a 'grace') of the Council of the Senate is opposed by at least ten

◄ **73** *Trinity College dining hall: a view of the interior showing the notable double hammer-beam ceiling. This hall was closely modelled on the hall of Middle Temple, London. The founder's portrait hangs above high table*

members of the Regent House there is a ballot. The discussions preceding any vote are published in full in the *Reporter,* the official weekly journal of the University. The Regent House also elects some members of the Council of the Senate. Of all the other British universities, only Oxford has a similarly democratic constitution.

Other important University officials are the Proctors, dons appointed by the University every year to represent the authority of the Vice-Chancellor and to discipline the undergraduates (i.e. students who have not yet taken a degree). They are much less familiar to modern undergraduates than to those of earlier generations; until the 1960s they used to patrol the streets after nightfall with the 'bulldogs', the bowler-hatted University policemen, looking for undergraduates infringing rules by being out after sunset without their gowns on. There is a special pro-Proctor who supervises the keeping of cars by undergraduates in the University. No undergraduate is allowed to keep a car without special permission from him. This helps to relieve the pressure of traffic on Cambridge's narrow streets, and it explains the great number of bicycles to be seen throughout the city.

The undergraduates themselves are selected not by the University but by the colleges to which they apply. Each college either provides teaching in every subject or makes arrangements to send its students to dons of other colleges for tuition in the less common subjects; the student's choice of a college may be dictated by its traditional reputation for his or her chosen subject (e.g. medicine at Gonville and Caius, law at Trinity Hall), or by school or family connections, or by a particular quality of the college such as size. In this last respect the range is wide, the largest colleges being Trinity (633) and St John's (510) and the smallest Peterhouse (205) and Corpus Christi (219); the average is about 390 (Emmanuel and Newnham) (figures are undergraduate numbers in 1985-6, and the colleges have proportionate numbers of research students and fellows). Most students apply for admission whilst still at school, some after they have taken their A-levels (final school examinations, taken at 17 or 18), so that they have a nine-month break between school and university; but an increasing number apply before taking A-level. Each candidate is interviewed by two or three dons at the college of his or her choice, and some are expected to take the relevant Sixth Term Examination Papers (STEP).

The University year begins in early October. There are three terms every year, each lasting eight and a half weeks, with an optional six-week term in the summer; but while lectures are given, and students required to be in residence, for only half the year, the dons use the rest of the time to do their own research. Most colleges are able to provide a room in college for their undergraduates for at least two of the three years which is the normal length of the undergraduate course. For the other year, the undergraduate has to live 'out', usually in a college-owned hostel or lodging house. Rooms in college range from luxurious 'sets' in ancient college buildings to small modern bedsitters. Each room has access to a 'gyp room' or kitchen providing cooking facilities (usually rather basic). 'Gyps' were college serving-men (known as 'scouts' at Oxford) who used to wait on the dons and students, bringing them meals and carrying coals for their fires. They have now almost completely disappeared, but most colleges still have women 'bedders' who clean and tidy rooms; they are traditionally supposed to be of advanced age and hideous appearance so as to present no temptations to the undergraduates they look after.

74 *Emmanuel College dining hall, with the tables set with college silver for a feast*

It is quite easy for undergraduates to base all their social life in college. They can eat all their meals in the (dining-) hall or buttery and use the college bar and Junior Combination (= Common) Room. Attendance at college chapel is no longer compulsory – as it still was in the early part of the century – but even the new colleges have their chapels, each with a dean and chaplain. A chapel service is one of the few remaining occasions when gowns must be worn; most colleges also insist on gowns for dinner in hall. In hall the master and fellows eat separately, on 'high table'; they usually have comfortable chairs, whereas undergraduates have to make do with benches. Dinner is candlelit in certain colleges, with a display of college silver on high table and traditionally a lengthy Latin grace before and after the meal (**73**, **74**). Dinner in the newer colleges tends to be more informal and democratic.

Every college has a master or mistress (but a provost at King's, a president at Queens', New Hall, Wolfson, and Clare Hall, a principal at Newnham and a warden at Robinson). He or she is usually an eminent academic, and although frequently involved in college committee work is unlikely to have much contact with the students. The senior members of the college, the fellows, are elected on the basis of their academic ability and publications. Most of them have heavy teaching commitments but in general regard their own research as equally or

more important. From amongst the fellows of the college each undergraduate has a tutor and a director of studies. The tutor looks after his or her social welfare, and is often asked for references or informal advice about careers. Some tutors establish close relationships with the undergraduates for whom they are responsible which persist beyond the student's University life. The director of studies is responsible for the undergraduate's academic progress. While lectures are organised by the faculties, the director of studies assigns his charges to 'supervisors' who give the students individual attention, teaching them singly or in small groups. Supervisors may be fellows of the undergraduate's own college or of another, or they may be research students. During his course the undergraduate usually has several supervisors, each specialising in a different area of the curriculum, though some directors of studies prefer to keep in close touch with their students by doing most of the teaching of them themselves. At the end of each term supervisors report on each pupil's progress to his tutor.

The daily timetables of undergraduates depend very much on their subjects. Those studying natural or medical sciences or engineering have their mornings (and often their afternoons as well) occupied with lectures and practical laboratory work organised by their faculty. In contrast, the students in most arts subjects can arrange their time more or less as they please. They have no essential lectures. For them the supervision, compulsory for all undergraduates, is by far the most important component of the course. Most undergraduates have on average one supervision a week for each part of their course that they are currently studying. A supervision is an hour-long meeting of one to six (usually two or three) undergraduates with a supervisor who sets his pupils

▲75 *Robinson College, Cambridge's most recent undergraduate college (opened 1980), was founded by David Robinson, a Newmarket racehorse owner, in 1974. The brick-clad building, designed by the Glasgow architects Gillespie, Kidd and Coia, faces onto a large and beautifully landscaped garden. The college presents a monumental, castle-like appearance to the street*

work for the coming week and discusses last week's problems and/or the students' written answers or essays. There are also less frequent classes and seminars for larger groups, organised mainly by the faculties.

Almost every undergraduate has to take an examination at the end of each year. At Cambridge each course is called a 'tripos' (e.g. the classics tripos, the geography tripos). The term is derived from the three-legged stools on which BAs in medieval times sat to conduct the oral examinations ('disputations'). Most triposes are in at least two parts ('Part one' and 'Part two'); the length of each part – one or two years – varies with each subject. It is possible to combine parts of different triposes, for instance to read philosophy for one year and then mathematics for two. Apart from the examinations at the end of each part of the tripos there are also preliminary examinations set by the University or the college. The results of tripos examinations are posted up on boards hung outside the Senate House, where they are keenly awaited by crowds of students. In most subjects successful candidates are divided into a first class (with 'starred firsts' for the exceptionally outstanding), upper and lower seconds (II.1 and II.2) and thirds; there are also 'special degrees' for those who fail altogether. The mathematics tripos preserves old titles for the different classes: wranglers (i.e. firsts) and senior and junior optimes.

The fortnight after the end of examinations is Cambridge's social season, 'May Week' (which actually takes place in June). The 'May Races' are rowed on the river (not on the Backs, but on the Cam beyond Midsummer Common) (**76**). This is the time of the traditional May balls, the expensive and formal

▼ 76 *College eights racing on the river in May Week. As the river is too narrow for boats to race abreast, they start at set intervals and attempt to catch and 'bump' the boat ahead. Here a bump has just been made, which the cox of the leading boat acknowledges with an uplifted arm*

college dances which last all night and end with the survivors punting to Grantchester for breakfast. Large numbers of plays and concerts are staged, many in the open air, and there are parties all day long.

Degrees are conferred in the Senate House in ceremonies known as 'congregations' (**77**). All undergraduates (or 'graduands', as they are by then) receiving degrees have to wear formal academic dress ('subfusc') with a hood trimmed with white rabbit fur to signify their BA status. Three years later, at another ceremony, they can become MAs, entitled to wear a hood trimmed in white silk. Doctors of Philosophy (PhDs) have scarlet hoods. These are the people who have stayed on or come from other universities – usually for at least three years – to do research in Cambridge's libraries and laboratories, and may subsequently acquire fellowships and lectureships. Postgraduates (i.e. those who have taken their first degree) account for about 19% of the whole University population; in 1985-6 there were 9702 undergraduates and 2333 postgraduates.

Although undergraduates are now far more concerned than they used to be with getting good degrees, it would be entirely wrong to picture student life as exclusive scholarship. For many undergraduates the friends they make at Cambridge are as important as the work they do there. They may have an all-consuming pastime: many give up most of their afternoons to sport, while rowers often have to turn out on the river at 6 a.m. once or twice a week. The highest University sporting accolade is to play in a match against Oxford. If this is in a 'major' sport such as rugby, cricket or rowing (the famous annual boat

▼ 77 After a degree ceremony in the Senate House, the new graduates and their friends and families gather on the lawn outside

race on the Thames) the athlete receives a 'full blue'; if in a 'minor' sport such as table tennis or ice hockey he receives a 'half blue'. The full blue is entitled to wear a pale blue blazer. The majority of sports players never aspire to this level but are content to play for their college teams.

There is a similar distinction between college and University in drama and music. For those happy to take part in the numerous college events these are no more than an enjoyable hobby; those who spend their time with the University Amateur Dramatic Club (the ADC) or with the Footlights (which stages a revue in the Arts Theatre each May Week) or with the University Musical Society (CUMS) may be laying the foundations of their careers. The ADC has its own theatre in Park Street and presents plays throughout the term. Other important University drama societies are the Marlowe Society (founded by Rupert Brooke), which once a year employs a professional director to produce an Elizabethan or Jacobean play at the Arts Theatre, and the Mummers, which every week during term-time stages small-scale plays by students or modern playwrights. CUMS puts on a number of orchestral concerts throughout the year, including at least one of large-scale choral and orchestral works in King's College Chapel. It is complemented by the Music Club, which concentrates on chamber and small orchestral works at its regular Saturday evening concerts in the University Music School on West Road.

Of all the many University societies (there are about 250 at any one time, with varying life-spans) the most famous is probably the Union Society. It occupies a large building of its own (an early work by Waterhouse) behind the Round Church where it stages debates throughout the term, mingling under-graduate speakers with eminent guests. The society is a traditional breeding-ground for aspiring politicians; in 1817 it was suppressed for discussing political subjects, but today, though it is sometimes uproarious, it is unlikely to be provocative. Less conservative undergraduate politicians aspire to office in the Cambridge Students' Union, which attempts to present undergraduate views to the dons.

Many of the events organised by the University and colleges bring together town and gown. Concerts and plays are generally open to the public; those given by the colleges usually take place in their halls and chapels or, during the summer, in their courts and gardens. Colleges also welcome visitors at their chapel services, of which choral evensong, held at least once a week during term-time in most colleges, makes a distinctive contribution to the life of Cambridge.

5 Places of Interest near Cambridge

Anglesey Abbey, Cambs. (D4, **79**). In 1926 Huttleston Broughton, later Lord Fairhaven, acquired the house, which incorporates the remnants of a 12th-century priory converted to domestic use in the 16th century. The son of a railway magnate and an American heiress, Broughton made extensive alterations and additions to house his huge and eclectic art collection, which ranges from works by Canova. Constable and Claude to 750 views of Windsor Castle. The luxurious ensemble has been compared to the interior of a millionaire's mansion on Long Island in the 1930s. The abbey's chief glory is its garden, one of the few in England designed on the grand scale this century. Avenues, spacious lawns, pools, shrubs, flowers and statuary are combined in a scheme that unites formality with charm and merits lengthy, leisurely enjoyment. A National Trust property.

Audley End, Essex (D6, **80**), is one of the country's greatest Jacobean mansions, although little more than a third of the original building remains. It was built by Thomas Howard, 1st Earl of Suffolk and James I's Lord Treasurer, between 1605 and 1614 on the site of a medieval monastery. It was on a giant scale – 'too large for a king', commented James I, 'but might do for a Lord Treasurer'. Christopher Wren justly noted in 1695 that it had been 'built after an ill manner rather Gay than substantiall'; maintenance costs were such a problem that in the 18th century much was demolished. At the same time the interiors were redesigned, partly by Robert Adam, who was also the architect of the Palladian bridge in the magnificent grounds, landscaped by Capability Brown. Other memorable features are the Great Hall, where a richly carved Jacobean screen faces a bold stone screen conceived by Vanbrugh *c*. 1708, a delightful Gothick chapel fitted out 1768-72 and grand apartments that enjoyably combine Jacobean and 18th-century decoration with Victorian standards of comfort.

◄ 78 *The nave of Ely Cathedral, looking west. The severe, sturdy arcades were begun c. 1110; they are almost totally undecorated. The western crossing arch was rebuilt in the 14th century to carry the weight of new additions to the tower. The wooden ceiling is a 19th-century replacement of a medieval original. Its paintings were begun by H.S. Le Strange and continued by Thomas Gambier-Parry, 1858-65. Gambier-Parry's son, the composer Hubert Parry, sat as model for one of the figures while on holiday here from Eton*

Bury St Edmunds, Suffolk (F4), is a delightful country town laid out on a grid plan shortly after the Norman Conquest. At its heart is the open space of Angel Hill, the embodiment of 18th-century provincial prosperity: Georgian houses and shops, the stately Angel Hotel (1779) and the Athenaeum and Ballroom (1804) face the splendid relics of the great Benedictine monastery around which the town grew up. Two massive and richly decorated gates, one Norman and one 14th century, lead to the extensive precincts, now a park; the ruins are not especially picturesque, except where Tudor and Georgian houses have been built into the remains of the monastic church's west front. Bury has two huge

late medieval churches: St James, now the cathedral, and St Mary, which has a famous lavishly carved hammerbeam roof.

There is much else to enjoy: the Theatre Royal in Westgate Street, designed in 1819 by William Wilkins, architect of Downing College, Cambridge (see page 34); the old town hall in Cornhill, by Robert Adam (1774-80), now an art gallery; and an impressive red-brick Unitarian chapel of 1711-12. Also in Cornhill is a Norman house, Moyse's Hall, now a local history museum. It contains relics of the celebrated murder of Maria Marten in the Red Barn at Polstead. Less sensational pleasures are offered by the Gershom-Parkington Collection of clocks and watches, in a beautiful Queen Anne house on Angel Hill.

The Devil's Dyke, Cambs. (D4), is a colossal bank and ditch approximately 7½ miles long, extending from Reach, at the edge of the Fens, eastwards to Wood Ditton, where once forest land began. The ditch has an average depth of 15 feet and ditch and bank together are about 110 feet wide. It was never a dyke, for it was designed as part of a system of defences blocking the Icknield Way, the ancient track between Wessex and East Anglia, and was intended to prevent invasion from the south. Other surviving parts of this system are the 3-mile-long Fleam Dyke, between Fulbourn and Balsham, and the slightly longer Bran

▲ **79** *The south front of Anglesey Abbey was built c. 1600 when the abbey buildings were converted to domestic use. The two-storied porch, bay window and dormers are typical of Jacobean manor houses. The porch is capped by figures of St George and the dragon, added in 1926*

Ditch, between Fowlmere and Heydon. These defences were the site of conflict, as the graves of soldiers on the Bran Ditch reveal, but the date of the 'dykes' is uncertain. Probably they were constructed by the British after the departure of the Romans in the 5th century, in an effort to protect themselves against the Saxons. Today they provide exhilarating walks across open countryside, and are rich in chalkland flora.

Ely, Cambs. (D3). The northern part of Cambridgeshire, the Isle of Ely, was originally an entirely separate area governed by the bishops of Ely; it did not finally lose its independence until 1965. The flat, open fenland is interrupted by areas of higher ground that were often surrounded by water before the drainage of the Fens was completed in the early 19th century. On the most prominent of these 'islands' is Ely, dominated by its magnificent medieval cathedral, which is visible for miles around. Ely is the capital of the southern Fens (as Wisbech is of the northern). It is a busy market town and was for centuries an inland port.

In 673 St Etheldreda founded a monastery here (probably near an existing Saxon settlement) which became immensely powerful. In 1083 the new Norman abbot began rebuilding the monastic church, which in 1109 became a cathedral. It was largely completed by the early 13th century, when the chancel was extended eastwards. The Norman nave (**78**), east transepts and richly decorated west front survive; one of the Norman west transepts collapsed in the 15th century and was never rebuilt. In 1321 the beautiful Lady Chapel was begun, but in the following year – on 22 February – the crossing tower caved in, badly damaging the Norman parts of the chancel, which had to be rebuilt. Fortunately the sacrist, Alan of Walsingham, was an architect of genius. He created a new, highly original octagonal crossing crowned by a high wooden lantern (**81**). This breathtakingly spacious design is one of the masterpieces of medieval architecture.

▼**80** *Audley End develops the elements of Anglesey Abbey's architecture on a palatial scale. The Great Hall lies in the centre of the entrance front, between the two porches. All this dates from c. 1610. The caps on the turrets are Jacobean, but the porches' parapets were added in the mid-1760s and the range behind the hall (in lighter-coloured stone) was begun c. 1753*

When in 1539 the monastery was dissolved, the cloister and many other monastic buildings were destroyed, although much was subsequently incorporated into the King's School. The Norman doors that led from the cathedral to the cloister remain; the richly carved Prior's Door of *c.* 1135 should not be missed. Prior Crauden's Chapel (early 14th century) is another monastic survival: it is tiny but lavishly decorated and has a very rare medieval tile mosaic pavement showing Adam and Eve.

Palace Green faces the west front of the cathedral. To the south is the mostly 17th-century Bishop's Palace, which incorporates substantial parts of the original late-15th-century building. To the north are some fine 18th-century

►**82** *Thatched, white-washed White Cottage, Grantchester. Timber-framed buildings are common in southern Cambridgeshire, although the wood is usually hidden under plaster. Reed-thatch is also common, because of the abundance of reeds in the Fens*

houses and to the west is the parish church, St Mary. Its vicarage, Cromwell House, was the home of Oliver Cromwell 1636-47. Down by the River Ouse, the cathedral is less dominant; once a port, this part of the town is largely given over to recreation. There is a local history museum in the High Street and an interesting stained-glass museum in the cathedral itself. On a clear day, visitors should take the opportunity to enjoy the spectacular views from the top of the cathedral's west tower.

◀ **81** *The interior of the lantern that surmounts the octagon of Ely Cathedral. The timber lantern's eight-cornered star vault has at its centre – 152½ feet above ground – a boss carrying a half-figure of Christ. The carpenter responsible for the erection of this engineering feat was William Hurle, who began work in 1334. The 19th-century painting probably preserves the original design of 1336*

Grantchester, Cambs. (C5), is a pretty village separated from Cambridge by beautiful water meadows. In summer an enjoyable afternoon can be spent punting out to Grantchester for tea. There are several attractive houses and thatched cottages (**82**) and the parish church has a very fine 14th-century chancel; the church clock was remembered by Rupert Brooke in his famous poem 'Grantchester', which nostalgically recalls the two years (1910-12) that he spent in the 17th-century Old Vicarage. Before that he lodged at the Orchard Tea Rooms, where honey is still served for tea. Byron's Pool, between Grantchester and Trumpington, has other literary associations: it is traditionally the site of the mill that forms the setting of Chaucer's 'The Reeve's Tale', and Tennyson had it in mind in his poem 'The Miller's Daughter'. The pool is named after Lord Byron, who used to come swimming here in hot weather when an undergraduate at Trinity College (see page 71).

Great Chishill Mill, Cambs. (C6, **83**). This picturesque open-trestle post-mill was built in 1819, using materials from the previous mill on this site, built in 1726. The area has several windmills: two of the best preserved are at Great Gransden and Burwell. 18th-century Downfield Windmill in Soham is maintained in working order and the milling process can be viewed when the wind is strong, and visitors can buy wholemeal flour ground in the mill.

► **83** *The post-mill of 1819 at Great Chishill, Cambridgeshire*

Hinchingbrooke, Cambs. (B3). The house is built on the site of an 11th-century Augustinian nunnery which in 1538 was given to the Cromwell family. Building continued through the 16th and 17th centuries. The result is an attractive exterior enlivened with bay windows on the north and a splendid bow window of 1602 on the south, topped with lavish cresting. The impressive gatehouse was moved here from Ramsey Abbey (also owned by the Cromwells) soon after the Dissolution. Its early-16th-century structure is decorated with carvings of wild men holding clubs.

Huntingdon, Cambs. (B3), still retains many traces of its great prosperity in the early Middle Ages, before the River Ouse deteriorated, hampering trade, and the Black Death devastated the town. All Saints and St Mary are the most substantial survivors of the sixteen medieval parish churches which Huntingdon once possessed. Earthworks of a castle are visible from the High Street. Other buildings of interest include the early-14th-century bridge over the Ouse, and Cromwell House in Ermine Street, where Oliver Cromwell was born. He was educated at the old grammar school (which Pepys also attended), now the Cromwell Museum. This 12th-century building was once part of the infirmary hall of the medieval hospital of St John. The poet William Cowper lived (1765-7) in the 18th-century house in the High Street now known as Cowper House.

Imperial War Museum, Duxford, Cambs. (C5). In 1976 the disused RAF station at Duxford was acquired by the Imperial War Museum. The airfield and its buildings are maintained as a museum piece, where exhibits too large for the IWM's home in south London are preserved and displayed.

Construction of the airfield began in 1917; it opened a year later and in 1920 became a Flying Training School. It was a fighter station from 1924 until it closed in 1961, and was the first RAF station to be equipped with the Spitfire (in 1938). During the Battle of Britain, the Duxford squadrons, led by Group Captain Sir Douglas Bader, inflicted heavy losses on German formations. From 1943 to 1945 Duxford was used by the United States Army Air Forces, whose aircraft based there provided fighter cover for the Eighth Air Force's daylight bombing raids.

Today most of the airfield buildings, which include three World War I hangars, have been restored, and nearly a hundred aircraft are on display. The substantial civil collection belongs to the Duxford Aviation Society, a charity which played a large part in restoring the airfield. Visitors can see extremely rare World War I aircraft as well as many World War II fighter planes of several nationalities. Most types of aircraft used by the RAF since 1950 are also here, but the most spectacular exhibit of all is not military – the British pre-production Concorde. Air displays and other special events are mounted throughout the year.

Kimbolton Castle, Cambs. (A4), is a mansion of the 16th and 17th centuries built on the site of a medieval castle and extensively remodelled for the 4th Earl of Manchester *c.* 1690-1704, first by Henry Bell, a King's Lynn architect, and then by Vanbrugh, architect of Castle Howard and Blenheim Palace. The result is a severely monumental composition that combines classical forms with the castle-like embellishment of battlements to make, in Vanbrugh's words, 'a very Noble and Masculine Shew'. Inside are enchanting wall-paintings by the Venetian artist Giovanni Antonio Pellegrini: moors, pageboys, musicians, parrots and monkeys are depicted in sparkling colour. The gatehouse (1765) is by Robert Adam. The castle has been a school since 1950.

Madingley, Cambs. (C4). The parish church and Tudor Madingley Hall make an attractive group at the centre of this pleasant village. The Hall was begun *c.* 1543 for John Hynde, a rich lawyer, and has been considerably enlarged and altered since, mostly in the 1590s and the 19th century. The grounds were landscaped by Capability Brown 1756-7. Edward VII, when Prince of Wales, lived here for a year while an undergraduate at Cambridge. Since 1948 it has accommodated the University's Board of Extra-Mural Studies. Just outside Madingley, on the St Neots road, is the American Military Cemetery (**85**), where almost 9000 US servicemen killed in World War II are buried.

▼ **84** *The Eight Bells Inn, Bridge Street, Saffron Walden. This 16th-century timber-framed building preserves its original upper windows. The plaster is simply decorated, but the wooden carving below the ground-floor windows is a lavish touch*

March, Cambs. (C2), is a small town extended greatly to the north by its railway yards. The parish church, St Wendreda, is perhaps the most spectacular in Cambridgeshire. Built mostly in the mid-14th and early 16th centuries, it has a magnificent double hammerbeam roof of *c.* 1500, unforgettably embellished with three tiers of angels hovering on extended wings.

Mildenhall, Suffolk (E3). The name of this pleasant town evokes a US airforce base and the famous treasure of 4th-century silver tableware found in a nearby field in 1942 and now in the British Museum. The east end of the splendid church is raised up above the High Street, proudly displaying the elaborately beautiful tracery of its east window (*c.* 1300). The chancel and north chapel of *c.* 1240-1300 are the oldest parts of the church, which is otherwise memorable for a set of sumptuous roofs. The nave has alternating hammerbeams and tie beams, decorated with tracery and angels. In the spandrels of the hammerbeamed aisle roofs are carvings, including scenes of the Annunciation and St George and the dragon.

Newmarket, Suffolk (E4). Roughly 2500 acres of heathland surround Newmarket and on any morning there may be up to 2000 racehorses exercising there (**86**). This is the capital of the English racehorse industry and has attracted monarchs ever since James I built a palace here for the sake of the local hunting (it burnt down in 1683). Charles II eagerly promoted racing at Newmarket: one of his horses, Old Rowley, gave its name to The Rowley Mile Racecourse. Race meetings are held at Newmarket between April and October.

Facing on to the long, wide High Street is the Jockey Club, founded in 1752 by a group of racehorse owners. It is now the industry's governing body and controls the licensing of jockeys and racecourses. Just off the High Street is the

covered sale ring of Tattersalls, where the public can attend auctions of race-horses, held here since the 1880s. The National Stud has been at Newmarket since 1967; it is open to the public on certain days in August and September.

▲ **86** *Racehorses exercising on Newmarket Heath on a chilly winter's morning*

Newport, Essex (D6), like Saffron Walden (page 101), grew prosperous in the Middle Ages by growing the saffron crocus, used for dyeing. It has several charming streets, and a·notable group of medieval buildings by The Green: Martin's Farm, which has a 15th-century exposed timber front, the Old Three Tuns, and Crown House, whose plasterwork was lavishly pargetted (decorated) with garlands in the early 17th century. In the main street is 15th-century Monk's Barn, which has exposed timbers and brickwork; it was once the summer retreat of the monks of the now-vanished St Martin's-le-Grand in the City of London. In the church is an extremely rare 13th-century painted chest; the underside of its lid is decorated with figures that include the Virgin, St Peter and St Paul.

Ramsey Abbey, Cambs. (B2). Like Hinchingbrooke (page 96), Ramsey is a monastic site given to the Cromwell family after the Dissolution of the Monasteries. Little survives of the abbey, founded in 969, for much of its stone was used to build several Cambridge colleges, including King's and Trinity. The most spectacular survival is the monastic guest house, built *c.* 1180-90 and converted into the parish church perhaps as early as the late 13th century. It has an impressive rib-vaulted chancel and a spacious seven-bay nave, lit by windows containing a large quantity of late Morris glass. The lectern has a

revolving top. The abbey's Lady Chapel was incorporated into the house built by the Cromwells in the 16th century. In 1737 this was bought by the Fellowes family, who employed Sir John Soane and later Edward Blore to make extensive changes. It became a school in 1937. The elaborate abbey gatehouse of *c.* 1500 (a National Trust property) also survives, although part was taken to Hinchingbrooke. On the ground floor there is a very beautiful monument to the abbey's founder, Ailwin, carved *c.* 1230.

Saffron Walden, Essex (D6), takes its name from the saffron crocus (*Crocus sativus*), which until the early 19th century was grown in the surrounding fields for the orange dye that it supplied. The crocus is shown on the town's coat of arms. Saffron Walden thrived on wool as well, and retains many reminders of its medieval prosperity. Chief among them is the stately church, rebuilt *c.* 1450–1525, in part by the masons Simon Clerk and John Wastell, who also worked at King's College Chapel. The tall octagonal spire was added in 1831 by Rickman and Hutchinson, the architects of St John's College New Building (see pages 65–6). Built on a small hill, the church commands many views in this most harmonious town. Medieval houses, built of wood and plaster, abound: note especially the exposed timbers and courtyard of the Youth Hostel, on the corner of Bridge Street and Myddleton Place. Many houses are enriched by pargetting (decoration of the plasterwork by incision or moulding). The most elaborate example is the scene of Thomas Hickathrift (a local hero) and the Wisbech giant on the former Sun Inn, which is part of a splendid group of 14th- and 15th-century houses on the corner of Market Hill and Church Street. Saffron

Walden has a good local museum, with displays of archaeology and natural history. On the common there is a famous large earth maze, of uncertain purpose and date.

St Ives, Cambs. (B3), is a pleasing riverside town which became prosperous in the Middle Ages because of its annual Easter Fair, granted a charter in 1110. The River Ouse is overlooked by the splendid steeple of All Saints, built on a large scale, mostly *c.* 1450-70. The town's most famous feature is its bridge, erected *c.* 1415, one of only three surviving medieval bridges in England with a chapel. This tiny structure, midway along the bridge, is dedicated to St Laurence.

Stretham, Cambs. (D3), is famous for its steam pumping-engine, built in 1831 for the Waterbeach Level Drainage Commission and today the only one of the Fens' pumping-engines to retain intact all its machinery and buildings (**87**). It was designed to drain water from the fenland into the Old West River, which now flows 4 feet above the surrounding land. Steam engines were introduced to replace the much less efficient wind-powered pumps; the first in Cambridge-shire was built in 1821 and by 1850 the county had at least 14. Stretham Old Engine is open to the public. The village's market square has a well-preserved early-15th-century market cross.

Swaffham Prior, Cambs. (D4), has two large churches side by side in a single churchyard (**88**), memorably raised high above street level. The older, St Mary, has an imposing Norman octagonal tower, capped by a 16-sided 13th-century stage. The 15th-century west tower of SS Cyriac and Julitta is also octagonal in its upper stages; the rest of the church was rebuilt 1809-11 and was for long ruinous. It is now in the care of the Redundant Churches Fund. There is an interesting set of Edwardian and later stained glass in St Mary, commissioned by the Allix family of 18th-century Swaffham Prior House, showing with documentary vividness the accession of Edward VII, a World War I trench and Wicken Fen (page 104), among other scenes.

Thaxted, Essex (D6), is almost a large village rather than a small town, but in the 14th and 15th centuries it was as busy and well-to-do as anywhere in Essex, with a thriving cutlery industry. This explains the splendour of the parish church, which has a magnificently tall spire (181 feet) and a wonderfully spacious interior. Some parts are 14th century, but most was rebuilt in the 15th century. The church is all-dominant, but visitors should not miss the timber-framed 15th-century Guildhall or, to the south of the town, a windmill of 1804 which is open to the public and offers excellent views. There are many half-timbered houses, often with jettied upper storeys (demonstrating their owners' wealth), and some with plasterwork prettily colour-washed.

Wandlebury, near Stapleford, Cambs. (C5), is the region's most impressive Iron Age hill-fort (**89**). It has a large circular ditch, approximately 1000 feet in diameter, with an external bank (there was an internal bank and ditch as well, added probably in the 1st century BC). At the centre of the fort are the stables (1708) of the now demolished mansion of the Godolphin family and the grave of the Godolphin Arabian, who died in 1753. He was one of three Arabian stallions

▶ **87** *The Engine House at Stretham, built in 1831 to house the steam-powered pump that drained this part of the Fens*

imported into England in the 18th century from whom almost all racehorses trace their pedigree. The site now belongs to the Cambridge Preservation Society and is open to the public. It is well planted, especially with beech. Wandlebury lies on the Gog Magog Hills, a low range to the south-east of Cambridge, said to be named after chalk-cut figures of the giants of Gog and Magog which were visible here until the 18th century.

Wicken Fen, Cambs. (D3), is Britain's oldest nature reserve, managed by the National Trust since 1899. It comprises 600 acres of artificially preserved wetland – the last undrained remnant of the Fens of East Anglia, which at their greatest extent, in pre-Roman times, covered 2500 square miles. The draining of the Fens has caused the peat surrounding Wicken to shrink, so windpumps have to be used to maintain the water level in the reserve: the opposite of the task for which such pumps were designed. Wicken Fen provides a habitat for numerous species of marsh-loving plants, birds and insects. Sedge and reed are still gathered here and there is a 2-mile nature trail (gumboots are essential) with a hide for birdwatching: warblers and breeding snipe may be seen. The Fens' history is explained in a permanent display at the William Thorpe Building, Lode Lane.

Wimpole Hall, Cambs. (B5, **90**), is the county's finest country house, an aristocratic mansion of subtle majesty. It was begun in *c.* 1640 for Sir Thomas Chicheley, but most of the visible structure is 18th century. The house was bought by Edward Harley, later Earl of Oxford, who in 1719 employed James Gibbs to design the splendid library and the chapel, which is elaborately frescoed by Sir James Thornhill. Other impressive interiors include the Book-

▲ **88** *The two churches at Swaffham Prior. In the foreground is the octagonal tower of St Mary; the 16-sided top storey and the porch are later additions. Behind it is the late medieval tower of SS Cyriac and Julitta*

room, the silk-lined Yellow Drawing Room and the plunge bath, all designed by Sir John Soane in the early 19th century. The 350-acre estate was laid out by Capability Brown and Humphry Repton and includes sham castle ruins north of the house, designed by Sanderson Miller, *c.* 1772. The most spectacular feature, however, dates back to the formal layout that preceded their work – the 2-mile-long south avenue, extending from the main front. Its elms, planted *c.* 1720, were killed by Dutch Elm Disease and have now been replaced by limes. Just to the east of the house is the church, rebuilt in 1749 and made gothic in 1887 (except for the north chapel, which is a 14th-century survival); it contains an outstanding collection of neoclassical monuments.

Wimpole was sold to Captain and Mrs George Bambridge in 1933. Mrs Bambridge, who was Rudyard Kipling's daughter, did much to restore the house; most of its furniture was brought here by her. In 1976 she bequeathed the entire estate to the National Trust, which has since re-created a formal Dutch garden in the grounds and restored Wimpole Hall Farm, built in 1794. The farm's Great Barn, designed by Soane, now houses a display of historic farm machinery and implements; the surrounding grass parkland is home for an important collection of rare breeds of farm animals.

Wisbech, Cambs. (C1), has been a prosperous port and market town since medieval times. It was at its peak in the 18th century, and a substantial amount of very pleasing domestic architecture of that period survives. The port was

▼ **89** *Wandlebury's Iron Age hill-fort, just outside Cambridge, today provides beautiful well-wooded walks*

always vulnerable to the silting-up of the River Nene, but engineering works from the 15th century onwards kept it open. Ship-borne trade in agricultural produce, for example, has continued, but on a reduced scale since 1847, when its importance was permanently affected by the arrival of the railway. There are several warehouses, some well maintained, but the chief architectural monuments to the old status of the port are the handsome 18th-century houses that line the north and south brinks of the Nene, creating one of the most memorable Georgian ensembles in the country. The showpiece is Peckover House (1727), now owned by the National Trust. It has much attractive plasterwork and woodwork and a Victorian garden with several rare trees, including a very large Maidenhair tree. Between the river and the church is Castle Estate, begun in 1797, a pleasant development of streets and crescents laid out around the site of a medieval castle. In the tiny Museum Square is the Museum of Fenland and Natural History (1846); as well as interesting local displays, there is a library containing a notable collection of literary manuscripts (which can be seen by appointment). Beyond the museum is the large church of SS Peter and Paul. It reached its present size in the 14th century, but much is earlier; note especially the late-12th-century north arcade of the nave.

▲ 90 *The south front of Wimpole Hall. The central block dates back to 1640, but was completely remodelled c. 1742; the lower ranges on either side are 18th-century extensions. The range on the right houses the chapel. The sculpture of Charity in the pediment and the chimney stacks were added in the 19th century*

PLACES OF INTEREST NEAR CAMBRIDGE

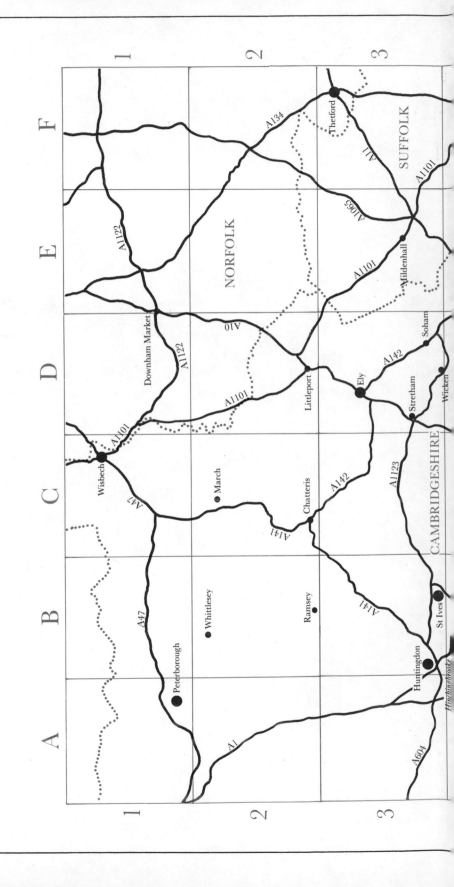